The Spirits of Lily Dale

The Spirits of Lily Dale

by Ron Nagy

with Joyce LaJudice

2013
Galde Press, Inc.
Lakeville MN 55044
www.galdepress.com

The Spirits of Lily Dale
© Copyright 2010 by Ron Nagy
All rights reserved.
Printed in the United States of America
No part of this book may be used or reproduced in any manner whatsoever without written permission from the publishers except in the case of brief quotations embodied in critical articles and reviews.

Second Edition
Third Printing, 2013

GALDE Press, Inc.
PO Box 460
Lakeville, Minnesota 55044–0460
www.galdepress.com

Dedication

I dedicate this book to Joyce LaJudice
and all the past and future Spirits of Lily Dale.

Contents

Acknowledgments	ix
Foreword	xi
Introduction	xiii
Laona, Chautauqua County, New York, 1844	1
Cassadaga Lake Free Association, 1879-1903	4
City of Light, 1903-1906	113
Afterword	132
Additional Photographs	134
Resources	175

Acknowledgments

Many thanks to Dr. Eileen McNamara for the
use of her postcard collection and vintage photographs.
Appreciation to the entire staff at Galde Press for the
great job in arranging this manuscript into a readable book.
And last but not least to Raymond Buckland
for his continued encouragement and support.

Foreword

This book is a condensed history that also includes personal commentary concerning the largest Spiritualist community in the world. I first compiled the history by searching through the notes and writings of our past historian, Joyce LaJudice.

Joyce labored for almost thirty years collecting camp programs, tax records, water bills, and playbills and saving news articles. She then spent thousands of hours at the local library researching through microfiche for any mention in catalogued news articles for Cassadaga Lake Free Association, City of Light, or Lily Dale.

Joyce diligently searched for any mention of an individual or event from the past and then cataloged the event that was significant to the continuous history of this religious association.

This book is not only about the early history of Lily Dale, but it is also about the past residents, guests, and the pioneers, exceptional people whom I call "The Spirits of Lily Dale."

Laona Train Depot

Introduction

Summary of Religious Movements in Western New York
Western New York, the burned over district
The New York Herald, June 16, 1869
—a faithful corespondent

One remarkable fact is again brought before us in this gathering of idealists and fanatics, and that is, that Western New York is the birthplace, home and refuge of the wildest theories and of all the isms that spring up to agitate society. Abolitionism, which has cost so much blood, brought upon us such a stupendous debt and jeopardized our republican institutions, grew up to be a mighty power there. Mormonism and its author, Joe Smith, were born there. John Brown was from that region. Communism at Oneida, on Lake Erie [Brockton] and at other points springs into life and flourishes only in that part of New York. Bloomerism sprung up there. It was at Rochester that the Fox family commenced their knockings and laid the foundation of modern Spiritualism. Indeed, there is hardly a phase of socialism, communism, religious fanaticism, political theory or agitation or of infidelity that is neither born or receives its growth in Western New York. This is a curious fact, and the philosophy or reason of it is a matter of interesting speculation. It has been said that this peculiar state of things may be attributed to the Welsh character of a great portion of the population, a great many Welch people having settled there originally. But there is a large New England and Old Puritan element there, and we all know that the Welsh were more superstitious and dogmatic than the Puritans. Western New York is a rich country naturally, is central, and once certain isms were started there followed another as a natural consequence until that region became a hotbed of them all, and of every new one that springs up. The only way to treat them is to let them alone, unless they become dangerous to the morals or peace of society, and they will die out in time through the progress of intelligence and march of a higher civilization.

Laona, New York, 1843, a Small Village outside of Fredonia
Animal Magnetism, also called Mesmerism—today we would call that hypnotism. Mesmerism was a new method of healing. A Dr. Moran from Vermont came to Laona to demonstrate Mesmerism…Dr. Moran healed a William Johnson who later was able to heal Jeremiah Carter, who also was able to go into a trance condition, identify objects [psychometry] and perform healing.

Weekly demonstrations were given…crowds came from all over Chautauqua County and beyond. Laona became one of the "stops" for what was then called "Itinerant speakers "[traveling lecturers]…Andrew Jackson Davis, Mary Davis, Dr. James Peebles, Elizabeth Lowe, William Denton, Warren Chase, and John Murray Spear were some of the most outstanding and well-known speakers who appeared there.

Simply stated, Spiritualism is a religion where the adherents converse with the so-called dead. Spiritualism is not a virus or a mental disorder as some books contend. Spiritualism was a movement that formed around the belief that spirits of departed mortals had begun to communicate with the living, and that the living could converse in a systematic way with the land of the dead.

Hydesville, New York, Thirty-Five Miles East of Newark

The Fox Sisters, Kate and Maggie, young teenagers, on March 31, 1848, began a first contact with a spirit, who, it was discovered through a system of raps, was murdered in 1843. This man was a traveling peddler who was murdered for the money he had been earning on his rounds of the countryside. It was further discovered that the name of the murderer was a man named Bell. The Bell family buried the peddler in the basement, and then moved away. The second family who occupied the house was named Weekman and they only stayed in the house for a year before raps started disturbing them. The spirit of a man had appeared and touched one of them. Out they moved.

Along came the Fox family who needed a place to stay while their house was being built. Little did they know that the house was haunted, and that they would also launch a religious movement that would continue into the twenty-first century.

That day of first contact with the spirit Charles B. Rosna on March 31, 1848, is called the beginning of modern Spiritualism. It was the end of old superstitions and the beginning of knowing and investigation. At Corinthian Hall, Rochester, New York, on November 14, 1849, the first public demonstration for the Fox Sisters was presented. After the Fox Sisters came forward acknowledging their ability to communicate with spirits, other people were bold enough to also admit to spirit contact. (A skeleton of a man was found in 1904 when a basement wall collapsed in the Fox cottage.)

Why did so many religious movements have their beginnings in western New York? Was it the isolation, solitude, and the vast areas of the frontier west of New England, New York City, and Boston? The proximity of the Great Lakes and large bodies of water can cause more powerful thought vibrations or more powerful weather patterns. Does it also help to be alone with your thoughts? New York was said to be the gateway to the West, and the fertile land attracted many settlers. The majority of settlers were of the younger generation, an age group of people in their twenties who were all open to new ideas and were disturbed by orthodox tradition. They had a solid Yankee heritage and exhibited a moral intensity. They were more sensitive to religious influences. The adolescent mind readily lends itself to religious excitement. Everyone awaited the millennium, and each movement had its own way or methods with various interpretations of a Bible. The older and more established generation stayed behind, content with what they had and where they were.

During the 1850s, a surprising number of Americans believed that the deceased could be contacted through trance mediums and séances. Many of the progressive leaders of the anti-slavery, women's rights, temperance, prison reform and labor reform movements were involved in Spiritualism and used it as a conduit for social and political reform. To them, Spiritualism was a scientific alternative to religious systems that they believed relied on speculation and dogma.

Anyone who attended a séance or Spiritualist gathering, and then was either convinced or impressed and talked about that phenomenon, especially an orthodox religious person of authority, was excommunicated and that person would then say they were a Spiritualist. Spiritualism grew by leaps and bounds, especially with the onset of the Civil War and the disruption of civil authority and ongoing so-called radical movements.

Western New York State was ripe for a new religious movement and the newspapers of the era took that as an advantage to market papers. There was no shortage of controversial discussions, and Spiritualism sold papers with the printing of spirit manifestations, rapping, materialization, spirit writing, slate writing, de-materialization, and apports.

For every honest medium there were at least two fraudulent mediums, people who were only showmen out for the money. Some of the best scientists of the day investigated the true phenomena, and some of that phenomena could not be explained away.

There were two kinds of mediumship: physical and mental. Physical mediumship describes something occurring that could be observed. The second type of mediumship, which was seldom found in newspapers, is mental mediumship. Mental mediumship is when the medium can sit in the light, contact and identify a deceased entity for whoever is requesting a "reading" (information) and give a message of some significance to the person requesting the reading. Mental mediumship did not sell newspapers nor did it generate a lot of money. Physical phenomena definitely got your attention, but the mental mediumship gave you positive assurance of the afterlife. Mental mediumship helped Spiritualism survive and continue to this day. Physical phenomena are frowned upon today for two reasons: (1) the physical phenomenon is easily faked, and (2) concentrating completely on the mental will bring in a higher vibratory rate of spirit entity and a more meaningful message.

During Victorian days women did not usually have a voice in public, but Spiritualism produced exceptional female trance speakers. Mostly women of little or no education, who could stand on a platform, would go into a spirit trance and lecture on subjects previously unknown to them. Almost every town and area had a Spiritualist organization or group of people who gathered together for meetings. Picnics and grove meetings were almost the same and could eventually become organized camps. Conventions were usually held at public buildings, with Spiritualists coming from all over the state and country for the purpose of organizing a national association with a common set of principles and declarations.

Seasonal campgrounds were arranged on private property. Committees were formed; a program was arranged and then some camps incorporated. During Victorian times camps were not uncommon. Almost 400 religious camps of various denominations were in existence in the United States by the late 1870s. Almost all religious denominations had a summer retreat, a camp. Spiritualist camps were no different except that they were more controversial—a gathering of intellectuals, religious dissidents, people who were considered radical's. Each group or individual had a distinctive speaking agenda with one thing in common—spirit contact—and guest speakers were invited to speak on platform. They could then influence large groups of open-minded individuals, which is why Spiritualists were called free thinkers. Men had long hair and beards, women short hair, and some women wore bloomers. Visualize a small city of tents with campfires burning, horses and carriages stabled away from the tent area, people milling about the campfires talking and discussing the latest news or national event of interest. Trees were cut in half-lengths for benches.

There were significant and recurring Spiritualist camp meetings and conventions in Western New York. To name a few, Laona 1843, Kiantone 1853, Progressive Friends of Human Progress (North Collins) 1857, The East Randolph Spiritualist Convention 1862, Johnson Creek (Lockport) 1867, Rochester Spiritualist Convention 1868, Buffalo Spiritualist Convention 1869, Progressive Friends of Human Progress (Waterloo) 1869, Mediums and Speakers Convention at Laona 1870, Alden Grove (Cassadaga) 1873, Watkins Glen Convention 1878, and finally the Cassadaga Lake Free Association (Lily Dale) 1879. Conventions were arranged for the purpose of agreeing on a common standard of principles or declarations. The conventions started in 1858 and were held in various states until 1893 when the National Spiritualist Association (N.S.A.) was formed. Today it is known as the National Spiritualist Association of Churches (N.S.A.C). This shows how difficult it is for Spiritualists to all agree. Free thinkers are fiercely independent people. It took thirty-five years of conventions to finally reach an agreement for a national association. A declaration of principles was not arrived at until 1899.

Hundreds, sometimes thousands, would gather at the camp meetings. Who was scheduled to speak, how well it was advertised, or how close to a major city it was, and ease of travel determined the number of people who would journey to the meetings. All the platform speakers at camp meetings were not Spiritualists. Camp programs did not specify what religion a speaker was or in most instances the subject of the lecture.

When Spiritualism started to progress, many people called themselves Spiritualists—as many as two or three million people—although many of the followers were not able to rid themselves of their previous orthodox religious beliefs. Some people around the country were treating Spiritualism as a hobby or pasttime, but Spiritualism at Lily Dale was the only religion. It was a way of life then as it is now. Lily Dale is to Spiritualism as Rome is to Catholicism. Lily Dale is the world's largest community that is dedicated to the religion of Spiritualism. Today much misunderstanding exists among non-Spiritualists, and distorted opinions still prevail to this day. Some people of other religions will not consider Spiritualism and are not open to reason, so ridicule is their only response. My hope is that this history and commentary will dispel any unfounded doubts about Lily Dale, Spiritualism, and spirit communication.

—Ron Nagy

Jeremiah Carter

Laona, Chautauqua County, New York, 1844

A Dr. Moran traveled from Vermont in the fall of 1844 to give a lecture and demonstrate animal magnetism or mesmerism in the village of Laona at Graham's General Store. Jeremiah Carter was in Dunkirk at the time attending his sick grandson and missed the demonstration. Jeremiah was also in the early stages of consumption and had especially wanted to attend Dr. Moran's demonstration. Many people attended the demonstration, one of them being William Johnson, the son of the local Methodist minister. At a later date Johnson, father of the future Marion Skidmore, proceeded to mesmerize Jeremiah Carter. On subsequent occasions during the mesmeric or hypnotic state, Carter could identify articles, give dates on coins, and perform other demonstrations that would interest those present. During Carter's trance state it was evident that an intelligence other than his own acted upon him. After a while Carter was able to enter into a trance without mesmeric aid.

During this time, Pitt Ramsdell found he also had the ability to induce trance. He also discovered that his niece Calphurina A. Ramsdell (later Mrs. A. A. Straight) was an excellent

Laona Church.

subject. She, like Carter, was afterward able to go into the trance state without assistance and demonstrate spirit communication. Soon weekly demonstrations were given in public meetings. Crowds increased, and soon people came from all over Chautauqua County to witness the events.

A Spiritualist society was formed at Laona in 1855 and was called the Religious Society of Free Thinkers. The Society purchased an old Universal Church for their meetings. Many noted men and women appeared on the platform in those early days. The eminent scientist William Denton delivered lectures on geology and the philosophy of Spiritualism. Later lecturers were P. B. Randolph, George W. Taylor, Andrew Jackson Davis, Mary F. Davis, Elizabeth Lowe, Cora L. V. Scott, Henry C. Wright, Warren Chase, Selven J. Phinney, S. B. Brittan, John M. Spear, and Lyman C. Howe.

Willard Alden, a member of the Laona Spiritualists, owned a farm along Middle Cassadaga Lake, about six miles from Laona. Alden used a section of his large house as a stopover for travelers who used the Frisbe Road Stage Coach. Alden and the Laona Spiritualists started a yearly "Spiritualist Picnic" on his farm in 1873. Each year it lasted an extra day, hosted guest speakers, and drew large crowds. In the spring of 1877, Jeremiah Carter of Laona heard an unseen voice clearly say to him, "Go to the Aldens and arrange for a camp meeting." This unseen voice repeated itself again very clearly. The next morning Jeremiah Carter walked the entire six miles from Laona to Cassadaga. Did Jeremiah walk that long distance so he could clearly consider how he was going to present this spirit command to Willard Alden?

Willard Alden gladly accepted the plan of a Spiritualist camp meeting being held on his grove and grounds, but the expenses of the lectures and provisions would be met by the Spiritualists. A committee was formed and a camp meeting was held September 11 to 16, a total of six days. Carter collected a fee of ten cents from each visitor.

Willard Alden passed to spirit life on February 25, 1878, and that year's camp meeting was held September 6–16. There was an added expense of $160 because Willard's son Theodore had the camp grounds fenced in. A fee of ten cents was still collected from each visitor. At the business committee meeting on May 17, 1879, Theodore Alden asked that a percentage of the gate receipts be turned over to the Alden heirs as rent. The committee was unwilling to do this because they had assumed the responsibility for the general expenses. Theodore Alden held to the percentage basis and the meeting was adjourned with a feeling of dissatisfaction and uncertainty as to the future.

Cassadaga Lake Free Association, 1879–1903

On August 23, 1879, persons held an informal meeting favorable to organizing a Camp Meeting independent of the Aldens and to secure new grounds. The object was to organize a corporate body under the New York State laws, for the purpose of buying land and conducting camp meetings. A committee was formed to draft by-laws and a subscription list was opened to buy stock.

The following persons subscribed for stock at this time:

Mrs. Kate McCormick
Mrs Almena Allen
W. P. Baxter
Freeman Lake
Thomas J. Skidmore
Benjamin Baldwin
Mrs. Mary Leach
David S. Ramsdell
George C. Rood
Martin R. Rouse
J. B. Hall
A. A. Straight
A. G. Purple
Abbie Cobb
Linus Sage
Lydia Sage
J. E. Holley
H. H. Thayer
Oliver G. Chase
Mrs. O. G. Chase
Albert S. Cobb
Martin H. Goodrich
M. J. Hull
N. N. Whitaker

The question of where to purchase real estate was brought up earlier. Several locations were suggested. Some favored

Chautauqua Lake, others Lake Erie, and still others Cassadaga Lake. A messenger was sent to Amelia H. Colby, who was requested to name the new association. She complied with "Cassadaga Lake Free Association" and the necessary papers for incorporation were filed with the clerk of Chautauqua County on August 26, 1879.

The Fisher family who owned the property bordering north of the Alden Farm was contacted and the first 20-5/8 acres of land along the east side of the upper lake in Cassadaga were secured for $1,845.12. The following Saturday September 5, work started with Albert Cobb, the association president, felling the first tree. Lot rentals or leases were set at three dollars a year with no lots to be sold outright. The grounds were surveyed for lots and the grounds were fenced in on three sides.

A fifty-by-eighty-foot horse barn was constructed at the far northern end of the property. Work "bees" were held, and one and all, men, women, and children helped clear the land. By 1880 the horse barn was raised one level and became the Grand Hotel. Hung suspension was a common method of construction in the 1880s. A new horse barn was built at the east end of North Street, again placed at the end of the property. During the season many more buildings were erected, including the building containing the ticket office and C.L.F.A. office at the entrance gate. A bridge, an all-wooden structure, was built, and a railroad depot was erected on the right side as you face the bridge.

On June 16, 1880, the Spiritualists dedicated the Cassadaga Lake Free Association to free speech, free thought, and free investigation Mrs. Elizabeth Lowe Watson and Mrs. Amelia Colby were the featured speakers. Mrs. Colby's train was late so Mrs. Watson spoke for two hours with an audience of 1,200, some sitting on cut tree trunks as benches around the "House of Boughs." The House of Boughs was a tent frame with tree boughs and branches, flowers, and vines to cover it. A crowd of three thousand could have been expected that day but for the threatening heavy clouds and rain. If it had rained, the ded-

First gate.

Elizabeth Lowe.

House of Boughs.

Melrose Park.

ication ceremony would have been held inside the Grand Hotel, which at the time was one large room equipped with seating.

The fifth annual Camp Meeting at Lily Dale, Cassadaga, N. Y., will commence on Friday June 3rd and close June 26, 1881.

Some of the ablest and most popular speakers on the continent are engaged among whom are Dr. J. Peeples, American Counsel and famous tourist. He has made two journeys around the world and is the author of many interesting books. He will speak as follows: Friday June 17, Sunday June 19 and 26 and during the week between the 19th and 26, he will lecture on his travels in Asia and Africa.

Also engaged are Mrs. Lydia Pearsall of Michigan, Judge McCormick of Fredonia, Mrs. C. Fanny Allyn, the famous improvesance and psychromestic test and glove reader, whose gifts so surprised and delighted those who heard her last year. Miss Jenny Rhind, the Symboltic medium and delaeter and Lyman C. Howe of Fredonia.

Jennie Rhind.

Auditorium under construction.

Lyceum, 15 North Street.

Just one year later the second floor of the Grand Hotel was finished and furnished, with lodging for forty persons. A score of cottages were built and lots were leased. More were wanted as soon as the lots were surveyed. Stock was selling for twenty dollars a share for future enlargements. Famous mediums and speakers from all over the country were engaged for the camp meetings. A lunch counter for cold food was added to the Grand Hotel, with hot tea and coffee.

Theodore Alden was still holding his Spiritualist annual picnics early in the month of June and calling them Lily Dale so as not to interfere with his picnics. (Cassadaga Lake Free Association held a picnic later in the month of June.) Then a week or two later he held the annual camp meeting. This caused stress between both camps. Scheduling and travel time for both mediums and speakers were difficult to arrange. The arrival of Mrs. Margaret Fox Kane caused a ripple throughout the camp, and Pierre Keeler spent his first season at Cassadaga Lake. A telegraph office was added to the gatehouse and finally Cassadaga Camp was connected to the outside world.

In 1883, J. B. F. Champlin was contracted to build a fifty-by-fifty-foot auditorium, enclosed on three sides and supported by pillars with curtains to be let down during inclement weather. A sixteen-by-forty-eight-foot platform to the rear was the stage. A bathhouse with hot and cold water was built at the beach.

The Alden House was enlarged, adding thirty rooms. The first water tower was erected across from the Alden House.

Theodore Alden stopped his annual picnics in 1884. No basis for this was ever given, although reasoning shows that Cassadaga Camp was investing a vast amount of money by selling stock and adding improvements continually as well as paying for the best speakers and mediums. Theodore Alden may have been strapped for money or had a change of heart, but records show he moved into a house within Cassadaga Camp.

Thomas Lees, a Spiritualist missionary who traveled the country starting children's lyceums, moved his class from a tent in the park to a permanent building, 15 North Street. Marion Skidmore, who collected books from the camp visitors each summer and saved them for the following year for other visitors to read, started a tent in the park—the original library. (Thomas Lee's tent and Marion Skidmore's tent were next to each other's across from where the Pagoda now stands.) The original House of Boughs was also in that area in 1880.

Eighty cottages were now built and occupied on the grounds. Six thousand people were in attendance to listen to Jennie Hagen lecture, and plans were being made to enlarge the auditorium again. Stores were situated behind the auditorium and would be in the way of this expansion. These stores were moved slowly to the area of the assembly office at the gate, forming a central shopping area.

The decision was made to expand Cassadaga Lake Camp Meeting again. The Patterson family was contacted so Cassadaga Lake Free Association could buy all the land from North Street, North to Cassadaga Lake, and to the east boundary line of the original purchase. The fifteen acres of land were agreed on for the price of $2,550 on October 18, 1887.

The land was surveyed for lots, and thirty cottages were erected before camp season of 1888 started. Construction was started and finished on what would be called Library Hall. A large all-purpose building would have Marion Skidmore's collection of books on the second floor, and the first floor would be used for séances, meetings, and classes. Cassadaga Lake now had enough year-round residents for the United States Post Office Department to recognize that the Spiritualist village needed a post office. The post office was established on June 27, 1888, and called Lilly Dale—with two *L*s. The train-depot sign painter had misspelled his sign and the post office assumed it was the correct spelling. It took until 1927 to have it corrected.

Cassadaga Lake could now boast a post office; a resident physician and surgeon (Dr. Hyde); a resident teacher, who would instruct pupils singly or in a class; an instructor on violin, piano, and organ; and two or three resident mediums. Cassadaga Lake was becoming quite a little "City in the Woods."

The Cassadaga Lake branch of the Universal Temperance Union was organized September 12, 1888, and a branch of the Political Equality Club was organized at Cassadaga Lake with Mrs. Marion Skidmore as its first president. The first Political

Equality Club was founded in Jamestown with Mrs. D.H. Grandin as its president. The first Political Equality convention held in the State of New York was held at the Opera House in Jamestown, October 31, 1888.

The tenth annual camp meeting opened on July 26, 1889, and quoting from the *Banner of Light*, a Spiritualist newspaper from Boston, the number of completed houses on the grounds was 108.

> Sixteen new ones were built since the close of last season. The Auditorium has a seating capacity of eight hundred and is a thing of beauty. The new Library contains a large lecture room and a library filled with progressive literature. It has several private rooms fitted for the use of mediums and professionals. The newsstand is a new building and is kept by our venerable brother Gilbert Purple.

The newsstand is believed to have been located where the Pagoda now is situated.

> A new school district has been granted and in the near future we hope to have a school and college that will do credit to the cause of truth and progress.

The school district was Pomfret district 6. The first schoolteacher was Harrison Barrett, and classes were held at the library hall until the schoolhouse was completed in 1890.

The Grand Hotel had an addition built this season (called "the wings"), and the kitchen was furnished with all modern improvements. The dining room could seat 150 persons and there were 119 beds on the upper floors.

> On Library Street the building of Mrs. H.T. Stearns is nearly completed. It is built in Octagon form, and when completed will be used for private meetings, lectures and a permanent home for the children's lyceum.

The Octagon building was either sold or gifted to the Assembly in 1892.

Schoolchildren.

Octagon House.

The South Park House was built on the west corner of Cleveland Avenue and Third Street, a hotel with twenty rooms on the second floor and a hardware store on the first floor. This building burned out in 1903 and was replaced with a stone structure by Fred Foote that is now called the Morris Pratt building.

The schoolhouse at the far end of Library Street was erected and finished in 1891 and ready for the fall school term. Two steamers, the *White Wing* and *R. S. Lillie* made voyages up and down the lake from Cassadaga Village to Cassadaga Camp several times daily to carry passengers from the dance halls in Cassadaga to events at Cassadaga Camp.

A meeting was held at the Octagon building by the Political Equality Club to announce that August 15 is to be set aside as Woman's Suffrage Day with the Rev. Anna Shaw, Susan B. Anthony, and Miss Hattie O. Pesate of Jamestown as speakers.

On Woman's Day the grounds were packed to capacity. Twenty five hundred tickets were sold at the gate. Everyone wore yellow and white buntings; star spangled banners and the suffrage badge for the cause they were here to celebrate. The Auditorium was packed to capacity and it was difficult to even obtain standing room within hearing distance of the rostrum. The Northwestern Orchestra played a patriotic selection; Mrs. Cora L. V. Richmond offered the invocation after which Harrison H. D. Barrett, chairman of the C.L.F.A., made a short welcome. Mrs. Elnora M. Babcock, president of the Chautauqua County Political Equality Club, in taking the chair, stated nowhere in the county were Suffrage Women so warmly received as in Lily Dale; and drew a sharp contrast between "tolerance" of Chautauqua Inst. and the cordial support of Cassadaga.

A Spiritualist Wedding

On Saturday July 11, Miss Jennie B. Hagen, arrived and was greeted with one united impulse of warm and tender affection.

On Sunday morning, the 12th, Mrs. R. S. Lillie gave

Jennie B. Hagen.

The 1898 ferris wheel, to rear is electric power plant, on right is the bowling alley (first floor) and pool tables (second floor).

her usual discourse, upon the platform were the Chairman, H. D. Barrett, Miss Jennie B. Hagen, Mrs. Clara Watson, of Jamestown and Mrs. Lyman (a speaker and medium who is en route for the East, where she has engagements for the season).

At the conclusion of her discourse, Mrs. Lillie very considerately dismissed Miss Hagen, and communicated to us the fact (which was no news to many of us) that Miss Hagen was contemplating matrimony, which was to have taken place very quietly in Buffalo the next morning—the newly married pair to proceed from thence directly to Jennie's home in North Framingham, Mass., her mother being to sensitive at the prospect of giving her beloved only child to the keeping of another. Though unquestionably a man in every way worthy of her, to feel that she could witness the nuptials. But we of Cassadaga Camp, feeling that we are next to her mother in affection and Spiritual relationship to Jennie, she being in a spiritual sense the child of our adoption had persuaded her to change her plans and be married here in this big family of salacious and loving hearts. The plan was approved and warmly responded to and on Monday was carried out to perfection.

There was only a single day in which to make preparations for the marriage and give her such as "send off" as our hearts desired. But on Monday every hand and every heart entered into the work as with a single impulse of love. Water lilies were gathered from the lakes and the fields, woods and lawns were rifled of their flowers and foliage and by a little past noon the rostrum and vicinity constituted a bower of tint and odor. A bell composed of pure white flowers on the outside and of green leaves and ferns inside, hung from the ceiling over the bride and groom; a table made of beautiful bright clover blossoms in the center of which were two white lilies, representative of the two pure lives about to be united, stood in front of the rostrum; wreaths, hearts and other ingenious and pretty devices of flowers and ferns were overhead and in every nook and corner.

Some little time before the appointed hour (2:30 o'clock) the auditorium was filled with beaming expectant faces. Miss Porter of Corry, Pa., presided at the piano, and as she struck up the wedding march the wedding party proceeded from the cottage of R. S. Lillie, down Cottage Avenue to the Auditorium. At the head was Mrs. Gaston (wife of President A. Gaston). Mrs. Lillie came next. Lillie and the groom, Bradford D. Jackson, whose bearing was that of a noble and manly man. Then the two bridesmaids, little Jessie Darte and Maude Calhoun arrayed in white and carrying bouquets of flowers. A. Gaston with the bride elect upon his arm brought up the rear. Mrs. Gaston and Mrs. Lillie came first upon the rostrum. The latter, whose face beamed with the inspiration of the hour, stepped forward, and gave a brief speech upon "Marriage as Viewed In The Light Of Our Spiritual Philosophy."

To a few notes of the wedding march the bride and bridegroom stepped forward, and Gaston performed the office of giving away the bride. As we looked upon her in robes of spotless white, the fleecy folds of the bridal veil falling about her with no adornments save those of natural flowers, we thought: yea verily, thou art the child of spirit! One whose face spreads a character of such loveliness, such purity and innocence, is a fitting companion and vicegerent of the angels, and we can but call them blessed.

As Gaston placed her hand in that of the groom he pronounced the following ceremony:

"Bradford D. Jackson: As a representative of Cassadaga Lake Free Association; as a worker in the field of reform to which this Lady's life has been dedicated: as a friend and acquaintance of hers in the years have passed; and in the name of the Spirit world, I give into your keeping Jennie B. Hagen and in giving I trust that you will not only cherish and protect her, but that you will aid in carrying forward this great work to which her life has been devoted; and as you assist her and the spirit-world in carrying out this may you be blessed in the union."

Then followed the spiritual part of the ceremony given inspirationally by Mrs. Lillie. One who had watched over Jennie from her childhood and opened with the following lines:

"By the powers that watch above you,
your hands are placed together
to tread the pathway of earth-life,
In storms and pleasant weather."

and broadened into a poetic portrayal of life, as we

find it, and the magical power of love in increasing the joys and lessening the ill which are the common inheritance of humanity. She then said:

"We shall not adhere to the old custom of exacting promises of obedience except by saying to you jointly: Will you in the presence of these witness and the Spirit-world promise to fulfill the obligations of husband and wife in accordance with the laws of this state?"

This being assented to by both, Mrs. Lillie continued: "Should we exact a promise of obedience from you, Jennie, we should exact it equally of both; but, in your case, obedience to a higher power is required of both of you."

"Now don't look so serious," said, "Boy White" (a humorous control which most of us are familiar with) "you have, both of you, got to mind us."

Then in a more serious vein the ceremony was concluded as follows:

"Now in the presence of these witness and the higher intelligences—in the name of love, the most divine power than which there is no higher—in the name of the Spirit world and of the intelligences which control your organism, and in the name of the Infinite Spirit, I pronounce you husband and wife."

Gaston then stepped forward and said: "By the power vested in me by the law; I also pronounce you husband and wife."

Mrs. Lillie remarked jocosity that they were now tied together in a double bowknot. Congratulations were extended to the happy pair, and the entire company proceeded to the hotel, where a sumptuous repast was served in the most approved and gratifying manner. and Mrs. Gaston occupied the seat of honor at the head of the table, with and Mrs. Skidmore on the right, the bride and groom at the left, followed by and Mrs. Lillie, Mrs. Judge Lott, Mrs. Rathburn and other notable workers in the cause of truth.

The Buffalo Express, August 24, 1892
Cause of Women
Bright Speakers at Lily Dale Yesterday
A Great Crowd Present

Mrs. Isabella Beecher Hooker presided and Susan B. Anthony and the Rev. Anna Shaw talk and what they said:

The Auditorium.

The 1894 post office, telegraph office, and CLFA offices. Left to right: Mr. Rouse, Mrs. Rouse, A. E. Gaston, Lyman Howe (?), Mrs. Howe, unidentified child, unidentified, Thomas Skidmore, Marion Skidmore, C. B. Turner, Mrs. R. S. Lillie, D. B. Merritt, Hon. A. Gaston (?), unidentified, Jack Lillie, unidentified.

The Lily Dale cottages were up bright and early this morning. From 8 till 10 o'clock it seemed though every woman in the camp was trying to get the best of every other woman in the way of decorations. Waving flags, evergreens, ferns, potted plants, trailing vines, Chinese lanterns, gorgeous sunflowers and yards upon yards of yellow bunting were everywhere lavishly displayed. Near the entrance to the gates two large banners were strung, bearing the inscriptions, "Political Equality" and "Lily Dale Greeting to Political Equality." The Auditor was gay with festooned flags, appropriate mottoes and a profusion of flowers and golden draperies. The platform was backed by a graceful showing of stars and stripes, through which were caught glimpses of green boughs and yellow draped pictures of Lincoln, Thomas Paine, Lucretia Mott and Elizabeth Cady Stanton. Staring the audience full in the face were large lettered inscriptions: "Government derive their just powers from consent of the governed" and "Woman's ballots mean enlarged opportunities for doing good."

Long before the hour appointed for the opening address standing room was at a premium. The meeting was called to order by Chairman Barrett, who welcomed the speakers and expressed himself as proud to wear the orange in their honor. He then resigned in favor of Mrs. Isabella Beecher Hooker, who presided throughout the day.

Mrs. Hooker said she was proud to have hailed from Connecticut. She was more proud of the fact that some of the blood of that grand old man, Thomas Hooker, who had framed the first written Constitution for the State that America had ever known, arrived in her children's veins. But perhaps after all, the Beecher blood was good blood to mix. She then called upon her audience to answer the conundrum, "If women are not citizens, what are they?" She begged women to consider their present situation and to dwell upon what the little white ballot had done for the African slave. The first speech she had ever made she had been called upon to say whether she would herself like to become an officeholder. She answered, "Yes! And I choose my office this very minute. I want to be Superintendent of Police in New York City." She declared that she had been running for that office ever since. When man comes to woman and put in her hand the magic symbol of freedom and says, "Come and help us," Then America will be saved. Mrs. Hooker introduced Mrs. Clara Burwick Colby, who lived in that great far-off west that could teach Eastern people many lessons.

Mrs. Colby had no new arguments, she said, to bring forward, but would as a few words to strengthen the faith of her hearers. She was assured of woman's progress every time she heard of a woman's day, a woman's union or a woman's club. Men spend far more time in telling women what they can't do than helping them to do it. They say, "See what you have accomplished without the ballot. We have done this for you." They forget how opposed they were to the innovations they now praise. The condition of women in Germany, who performed manual labor while yoked with oxen or harnessed with dogs, or those in the far East, who dared not walk the streets unveiled was scarcely more deplorable than patriotic working woman of America, who were governed without consent and taxed without representation. Buckley at Chautauqua recently laughed at the idea that women were slaves. "Jesus said nothing to Martha about being a slave." But on the other hand, neither did he say anything to Lazarus about being a slave. Yet if the learned doctor were occupying the same position as Lazarus did he would be apt to rebel against it.

The speaker then passed to the present state of things in Wyoming. This State in Anti-suffrage days was known to be notoriously lawless. But when women were placed upon the grand jury gamblers, law-breakers and demimonde fled the town. The chief objection to women serving as jurors came from men who held up the picture of one woman sitting up all night with 11 men. An incident was related of where six women and six men were sitting in judgment upon a man accused of a capitol crime. The bailiff took the six women to one room and the six men to another. The women, realizing the gravity of the situation, knelt in prayer. The men spent their time in playing cards and drinking whisky. Which six would be most capable of bringing in a just verdict? If women find unpleasant facts about jury serving they would alter them. She wrote to a woman juror in Washington to know how she liked her job. She replied "first rate. I never earned $3 a day so easily in all my life before." The speaker suggested that if there were more jobs of this kind women could give their husbands a Christmas present once in a while without the regulation newspapers joke about where the money came from. Arguments were brought forward to prove that woman as police justices gave satisfaction and seldom or never had a case appealed. The fear of men in general that the ballot for women would destroy native delicacy and home relations was unfounded. It had so proved in Wyoming the Democrats voted against the Territory being enrolled as a state because of its suffrage laws and it had kept them pretty busy ever since to explain to the feminine voters there that they had been in favor of women suffrage all the time. Politicians no longer dared put up an immoral candidate. They publicly acknowledged that the influence of woman's vote in Wyoming had been to lessen crime. Are the women of New York less free to be trusted than those in Wyoming? The laws of that State protecting virtue were the strictest in existence.

The article continues but the copy on hand was in such bad condition it could not be transcribed.

A matter of great interest to the public in 1893 is the fact that the system of water-works is being extended for the purpose of fire protection, and to furnish a supply of water in all cottages desiring it. In all about $10,000 have been expended this year in improvements. The money to carry them on has been furnished by the Board Of Trustees and other faithful friends of Cassadaga, among whom are The Skidmore's, Mrs. A. L. Pettengill, Hon. A. Gaston, H. W. Richardson, D. E. Bailey and Mrs. C. H. Henderson. Sewers have been put in all over the camp. The arc and incandescent lamps, which are hung among the trees, are in place. Delightfully pure, cold water can be obtained from numerous artesian wells.

A New railway station is just finished, providing ample accommodations for the crowds who arrive daily by all trains. In July construction was being done on the powerhouse and by the end of August was generating electricity. Records show 215 cottages on the grounds with 40 leaseholders living here all year round. A new and commodious depot is being erected by the New York Central and travelers will no longer be scorched by the August sun or pelted and frozen by winds and storms.

Mrs. Pettengill, the new member of the Board, in her largesse of heart and great love for the cause dear to us all, has with open and bountiful hand, dispensed beauty and utility on every side. Through her means the hotel has been renovated from bottom to top, newly painted, papered and carpeted. She has made the entire house beautiful and attractive; dining room is especially inviting in its tinting 1/2 pale green and buff, its curtains of spotless muslin and its ornamentation of ivy and basket flowers.

Through the generosity of our worthy President, A. Gaston and Mrs. Henderson of Erie, Pa., the necessary funds to carry out the work of putting in sewage and water-works have been furnished, and the camp is rejoicing in that and many other sanitary improvements.

A meeting of the National Delegate Convention of Spiritualists of the United States of America was held at Chicago, Illinois, September 27, 28, and 29, 1893. It was at this convention that the National Spiritualist Association was formed—now known as the National Spiritualist Association of Churches. As a result of this convention Spiritualism was registered in Washington, D.C. as a Religion. The National Spiritualist Association when formed used Lily Dale's Constitution and Bi-Laws and the sunflower seal.

On Wednesday June 7th, it was my good fortune to find everything in readiness of opening exercises of the Summer School of Psychic Science in the Octagon Building, two sessions of which were held on the first day and two on the day following.

Many great improvements have been made since last summer, among which must be noted, the refurbishing of the Grand Hotel, the erection and opening of many new and beautiful cottages, new seats in the parks, which are also far better wooded and more resplendently abounds with lovely flowers of all—the complete system of electric lighting which now illumines the grounds and Auditorium to perfection.

The Hotel now accommodates guests at one dollar per day, and upward, according to size and location of room, by the week, till July 20th, after which date the rates will be necessarily higher.

A matter of great interest to the public is the fact that

the system of water-works is being extended for the purpose of fire protection, and to furnish a supply of water in all cottages desiring it. In all about $10,000 have been expended this year in improvements. The money to carry them on has been furnished by the Board Of Trustees and other faithful friends of Cassadaga, among whom are The Skidmore's, Mrs. A. L. Pettengill, Hon. A. Gaston, H. W. Richardson, D. E. Bailey and Mrs. C. H. Henderson. Sewers have been put in all over the camp. The arc and incandescent lamps, which are hung among the trees, are in place. Delightfully pure, cold water can be obtained from numerous artesian wells.

Through the generosity of Mrs. Everett (daughter of Mrs. Pettengill) a very powerful and melodious organ now takes the place of the instrument, which formerly moved to and from the Auditorium and the Octagon building. On June 9, 1893, the first sewer pipe was laid and on July 31st cottages began connecting into the lines. In July construction was being done on the powerhouse (near the beach area) and by the end of August was generating electricity. Records show 215 cottages on the grounds with 40 leaseholders living here all year round. Leases were three dollars a year for ninety-nine years.

As the visitors move towards the C. L. F. A. grounds great changes meet the eye at every hand. The unsightly swamp has been filled in and a good plank walk reaches from the depot to the grounds. The old gate is displaced forever and a handsome Iron Gate surmounted by an arch upon which is emblazoned the letters C. L. F. A. has taken its place.

From that time to the present the growth of the camp both in a material and spiritual sense has been truly phenomenal. A stranger, especially if he be a poet or artist, might fancy, on entering the gates for the first time beholding the wondrous beauty of scenery, which meets the eye on every hand, that is a fairy isle dedicated to the gods. The labyrinthine walks, the flower-gemmed parks and multiplicity of shady nooks, the charming trio of lakes, their verdant banks stretching outward and upward until lost in the mazy hills, the groves and grand old trees which dot meadow and hills, which in the distance seem to touch the sky, the sweet, pure air and constant carol of birds- all conspire to drive dull care away and lead one to forget that there is an outside world where sorrow, want, ignorance, misery and strife are running rampant and driving men to very frenzy, causing murders, suicides, riots, and crime of every description.

A livery stable, supplied with fine horses and a variety of equipages, affords opportunities to those who wish to drive.

Sail and rowboats can be hired for a small sum, and fine steamers ply the lake between the camp and Cassadaga village every hour.

Bicycling, which has become a fad the world over, is no exception at Cassadaga. These with fishing, rowing, croquet, lawn tennis, toboggan slides, baseball, and the semi-weekly dances in the large cool auditorium, while the Northwestern Orchestra discourses, inspiring music—leave nothing lacking in making the sojourn of the pleasure-seeker a content and varied delight.

In spite of hard times, struggles, strikes and disasters, the opening day at this sylvan Camp excelled in numbers in manifest interest any that have preceded it. In the after-

Fishing at Cassadaga.

noon ninety-four more persons assembled in the Auditorium than were present at the opening year.

Prof. H. D. Barrett, whom we are so fortunate as to again secure for our chairman, opened the season with a few well-chosen and earnest remarks. All phases of phenomena have their representatives; it is said that there are eighty mediums upon the grounds; and while their manifestations are challenging the careful attention of investigators, we find the philosophy taking the deeper and broader hold on the minds of older Spiritualists.

During the past week it has seemed that "organization" has been in the very air at this Camp. At one of the conferences in which had been quite a heated discussion upon the subject, our venerable co-worker, Jeremiah Carter who is now over eighty years of age—and through a man of sterling sense and sound ability, has been modest to come upon the rostrum and offer his valuable thoughts to the public—surprised everybody by walking firmly and determinedly to the platform, evidently feeling he had something to say and that it was his duty to say it. He first gave a brief rehearsal of his career as a medium and healer, which we prefer to relate in our own way, as we would like to state a few facts which Dr. Carter left out, and which we deem essential to a just account of him. Considerably over forty years ago, contemporaneous with A. J. Davis's debut as a seer, there was considerable agitation in Laona, the home of Dr. Carter, upon the subject of mesmerism, and in some experiments made by the late George C. Rood, he found that Dr. Carter was an easy subject, and he was frequently mesmerized by Rood, the experimenter. After a while Dr. Carter found that the so-called mesmeric condition could be induced by holding a horseshoe magnet in his hand; and later, that he (Dr. Carter) could pass into that state at will. When in this condition things were said which were beyond the capacity or knowledge of Carter, and the intelligence thus manifesting declared himself as Dr. Hedges, an old physician of Chautauqua County.

One of the pleasant happenings of the camp during the past week was a visit by that renowned platform medium, John Slater late of Cleveland, Ohio, formerly of San Francisco, Cal. Slater was accompanied by

Thomas Lees of Cleveland, who was formerly connected with this camp. Slater gave a séance in the Auditorium while here, which was largely attended and highly appreciated.

Edgar W. Emerson has been with us during the past ten days, and has followed each lecture with his remarkable séances, which have, if possible, been better then before.

Vichard Ghandi, the Jainist philosopher and Hindu scholar, arrived at this camp on Friday; the 3rd, and caused quite a ripple of curiosity by his imposing manner and Hindu costume. Ghandi was one of the several delegates to the Parliament on that ever-memorable occasion of the Colombian year.

And Mrs. B. B. Hill and M. E. Cadwallader of Philadelphia fame has been here several days; Mrs. Cadwallader is doing an earnest work in the interest of "Antiquity Unveiled" and the National Spiritualist Association.

"It was voted that a reception room to the bowling alley be built two stories high and a sufficient size as to accommodate four billiard tables."

The Cassadaga Lake Free Association held a meeting of the stockholders Monday morning, the 20th inst. The old board was reinstated without a dissenting voice. On the contrary, a unanimous vote of thanks was tendered them for their faithful and most excellent management during the term of their office. Hence the Board of Trustees for the ensuing year will be:

Hon. A Gaston, of Meadville, Pa.; T. J. Skidmore of Lily Dale, N. Y.; M. R. Rouse, Titusville, Pa.; Mrs. Marion Skidmore, Lily Dale, N. Y.; Mrs. A. L. Pettengill, Lily Dale N. Y. The Hon A. Gaston was chosen to act as President, T. J. Skidmore as treasurer and A. E. Gaston as Secretary.

The acting Board of Directors were at this meeting empowered by the unanimous vote of the stockholders to purchase six acres of ground lying between the camp and railroad; also increase the stock from $20,000 to $40,000. The outcome of which was the selling of 160 shares of Cassadaga stock, sixty of which were taken by the Pettengill family.

"Woman's Day" was celebrated at Lily Dale on Aug

Susan B. Anthony.

22nd. Over Two thousand people arrived on the regular trains, and presumably another thousand upon the excursion trains.

Flags and yellow ribbons and buntings were floating from porches, balconies, windows and every place where there was room to put them: and the man or woman who minus the suffrage badge was below par in the estimation of Lily Dale.

Chairman Barrett opened the session by a well-worded address of welcome to the suffragists who had come to Cassadaga for their annual celebration. He said the suffrage movement was born the same year and simultaneously with the Rochester knockings, the beginning of Modern Spiritualism, and that Spiritualism embraced every movement that for liberty and equal rights.

Mrs. E. R. Clark of Stockton was then introduced as the Chairwomen of the day, made a well-worded reply to Barrett's address of welcome.

Miss Susan B. Anthony was then introduced. She said she was glad to be here at this camp, which has always been abreast in every work of reform. If as much had been done by the Methodists, Baptists or Episcopalians as had been done by the Spiritualist, there would not have been paper enough or ink enough or tongues enough to have written and spoken their praises. "But," said she "it is impossible for us to offer our thanks to Spiritualists without being doubly dammed for they are just as unpopular as the suffragists. Miss Anthony spoke of the defeat of the woman's suffragists before the State Convention the present year, at which time a petition of half a million names was presented. She termed it a Bunker defeat, not a Waterloo defeat—which means that they are gathering up their forces for a reorganization and attack on the Legislature, and that they expect to win.

The audience was swelled greatly beyond the capacity of the Pavilion in the afternoon and round after round of applause was given Rev. Anna Shaw as she poured forth eloquence logic and witticism. She said she always liked to stand upon the Cassadaga platform, for she felt perfectly safe. "There is no penalty for heretics in Lily Dale" said she, "and you couldn't turn me out of your church if you wanted to."

The famous North-Western Orchestra discoursed its most soul-stirring selections and the choir sang patriotic airs. Upon the rostrum were many veteran suffragists and Spiritualists, who, it had been discovered, go hand in hand on the march of progress. Among them were Mrs. Marion Skidmore, Mrs. Dr. Sarah Morris and Mrs. Sarah Anthony Bruits, The oldest living Suffragist and Spiritualist. Three thousand tickets were sold during the day.

At the grand dance in the Pavilion in the evening the women reigned supreme. One hundred and fifty dance tickets were sold and the grand march in the beginning, headed by Miss Anthony and Miss Shaw, was a pretty sight.

On October 3, 1893, Theodore Alden and his wife Angeline sold the Alden house and grove to John and Inez Agnew. On December 31, 1894 Abby Louise Pettengill purchased the property and on January 2, 1895 it was recorded in Mayville.

The sad news came one day that our beloved Mrs. Marion Skidmore, who was on her way home from Florida, on account of illness, was taken violently worse and was

Marion Skidmore.

compelled to stop at Cincinnati. Her husband T. J. Skidmore was with her, and on Saturday Feb. 2, all the relatives were summoned. On Sunday morning at 9:45, her spirit quietly left the mortal form.

The remains were brought to Lily Dale and the funeral services were held at the Skidmore home on Wednesday noon, the 6th 1895. Mrs. R. S. Lillie assisted by Mrs. Clara Watson of Jamestown, officiating. A large funeral cortege accompanied the remains to Fredonia, where they were laid in the family lot in Forest Hill Cemetery. Hon. Oscar W. Johnson, a brother of Mrs. Skidmore is now the only one left of a large family.

It seems impossible that dear Mrs. Skidmore has gone from our mortal sight forever. I loved her. She was the light and life of Lily Dale. How we all who impartially shared in her kind thoughts, will miss her! And on Woman Suffrage Days—can it be possible that the noble, motherly woman will be no more there to preside over it? And yet, when I think of the belief or knowledge, as she would say, of so many of her dear friends, that she is not gone, but with them in fuller sense than ever, I am led to exclaim, "Verily Spiritualist eat of bread the world knows not of."

Yours sincerely,
Susan B. Anthony

Banner of Light, June 29, 1895

On the eastern shore of the upper of three beautiful lakes sits Cassadaga—beautiful, entrancing and inspiring. The name has its derivation from the dialect of the Seneca Indians, and means "the lake under the rocks." It is about eight miles from Lake Erie and twice the distance from Lake Chautauqua. Being eight hundred feet above the former lake, it is desirable as a health resort, while the beautiful surroundings cause it to be a charming place is every way for a summer home. Add to these two attractions that of the spiritual, and it goes without saying that the place has a most perfect rounding, and is without a superior of its kind in the world.

This camp ground found its emanation in the Spiritualistic movement in the town of Pomfret, about forty-five years ago when William Johnson, the father of Marion H. Skidmore, and a small band, after witnessed manifestations in mesmerism and raps, started to form the Laona Free Association, which in 1879 became the Cassadaga Lake Free Association, formed after many meetings had been held, and great care taken with a view to success, harmony and up building of the cause of Spiritualism. Thomas J. Skidmore the husband of Marion H. Skidmore, was quite prominently concerned in the inauguration of the new movement, and continued his interest when the Cassadaga Association was formed and ever since that time.

The dedication of the grounds took place June 15, 1880, Mrs. Elizabeth Lowe Watson making the address, which was one of great significance. Every attendant alive today will remember the beautiful improvisation at the close entitled "The Water Lily." They will also remember the impromptu speaker's stand between the hotel, then in progress of erection and the lake.

The first cottage was built by Linus Sage, who with Lydia Sage had taken great interest in the new Association. Others soon followed, a ticket office built, and a large pine tree was felled and converted into seats for the audience in front of the speaker's stand. The hotel was ready for occupancy in August, and and Mrs. C. B. Turner found quite a number of willing guests, though the lack of market commodities made the undertaking quite formidable. It is worthy of note that W. J. Colville was one of the first arrivals.

The August meeting was held in the hotel, O. P. Kellogg, Mrs. A. H. Colby, J. Frank Baxter, W. J. Colville, Dr. S. B. Spinny, Giles B. Stebbins and Mrs. H. Morse taking part. The first year's work exceeded the expectations of the Association, financially and otherwise.

The second opened August 6, 1881, with Warren Chase, J. Frank Baxter, Thomas Lees, Mrs. Cora L. V. Richmond, Mrs. R, S. Lillie, Mrs. Nellie Bringham, and others. Mrs. Skidmore's grand work began to be felt more this season than ever before, and from that time to passing away, February 3rd, 1895, her interest in Cassadaga was pronounced in the fullest expression of the term. A. S. Cobb was re-elected President, Mrs. Skidmore Vice President, Skidmore Treasurer, and J. W. Rood Secretary.

The children's Lyceum was started this year by Thomas Lees and his sister Tillie Lees, and it has always been one of the most important features of the camp.

The grounds were further cleared this year, O. P. Kellogg was appointed to arrange for speakers, Mrs. Joan Carter and Mrs. Elisabeth purple having served the first and second years respectively.

It is useless to state in detail all the events of this year. President Cobb resigned his position, which was reluctantly accepted. T. J. Skidmore was elected. Cobb had done a great work in the up building of Cassadaga, and it was his influence as much as that of anything else, which gave life to the new enterprise. He is certainly entitled to great praise and here we find Mrs. Skidmore very active. Skidmore being away much of the time, duties fell upon her, and well did she perform them.

The third year saw most eminent talent upon the platform, and the names of Hudson Tuttle, Prof. Bradford, Mrs. Amelia H. Colby, O. P. Kellogg, Giles B. Stebbins, Mrs. R. S. Lillie, Mrs. Clara A. Field, Mrs. Clara Watson, J. Frank Baxter, need only to be stated as evidence of ability on the past of those participating.

In 1883 it was decided to build the present auditorium, and it was occupied in August of that year. The speakers were of the same distinctive class, and the interest in the meetings increased. The attendance grew very fast; improvements were made on the grounds in the line of new roads; President and Vice President Skidmore were re-elected and Thomas B. Buel who had succeeded Rood as Secretary, was succeeded by Miss Ida M. Lang. C. B. Turner was made Superintendent of the grounds, and has held the position consecutively with fine acceptance. Miss Hattie Myers was placed in charge of the Lyceum this year.

The 1884 meeting was also a fine success. O. P. Kellogg, who had been Chairman for five years, declined reappointment.

Athelson Gaston, who became interested in the camp in 1881, entered the Board of Trustees this year. Skidmore was re-elected President and Treasurer; E. W. Bond became Vice President, and Miss Lange Secretary.

The annual meeting of the stockholders of this year gave boom to Cassadaga of which it was in need. The time had come when pioneering must give way to civilization, and the enterprise from that time to the present has been a series of marked successes. The election of Gaston to the office of Trustee showed great foresight, as he has been a tower of strength to the place.

In 1885, Lyman C. Howe presided at the summer meetings, fine speakers taking part. Music was made more of a feature this year than ever before. Mrs. M. E. D. Sperra had charge of the Lyceum. The old Board of Trustees was elected, Rowe being substituted for Frank.

In 1886, larger numbers came to the meetings, and fine lecturers and mediums were in attendance. George W. Taylor and R. S. McCormick presided. Mrs. E. W. Tillinghast had charge of the Lyceum. The same Board Of Trustees was elected, and a library founded by Mrs. Skidmore, aided by many earnest workers.

The library was first located in a tent a short distance north of the amphitheater, but is now in a more substantial place. It has been a source of much entertainment and instruction. Friends have principally donated the books, but many have been purchased from a fund raised for that purpose by Walter Howell. Miss Lang resigned as Secretary this year, and M. J. Ramsdell was elected for the un-expired term.

The meeting of 1887 lasted from July 30 to Sept. 4, a week longer than ever before, the speakers including some of the best in the country. The stockholders voted to add to the grounds, and eighteen acres were purchased. At the annual meeting in September, Skidmore refused re-election as President, and A. Gaston was elected. Skidmore retained the treasurer- ship, and A. E. Gaston was elected as Secretary.

Early in May 1886, J. W. Dennis was chosen a Trustee to fill the vacancy caused by the passing out (death) of Rowe. In 1888 the meeting was a grand bag.

The old Board was re-elected, and no changes made in the officers, which was also true of the following years down to the present, with the exception of a few instances.

Good speakers have always been a rule at Cassadaga, and the interest has increased each year. From the humble beginning the increase has been great. There are now hundreds of cottages, many other buildings have been erected, the Association property added to constantly, and the grounds made an independent school district. Cassadaga is without question one of the most interesting camps in the world.

With that has been said, it is necessary to visit this charming spot, not only to inspect its beauties, but to get in touch with the noble hearted men and women who are interested there. Spiritualism has many true followers at Cassadaga—followers who allow neither expense nor breadth of opinion to circumscribe their efforts. Their names will live after they have gone from the material to the spiritual realm. One has only to breathe the name of Skidmore, and the memory is flooded with thoughts of services well performed.

The present officials are H. W. Richardson, East Aurora, N. Y.; T. J. Skidmore, Lily Dale, N. Y.; A. L. Pettengill, Cleveland, O.; M. R. Rouse, Titusville, Pa.; D. B. Merritt, Linden, N. Y, A. Gaston, Meadville, Pa., Trustees.
Banner of Light, September 14, 1895

The Closing Week at Cassadaga Camp

On Sunday, Aug. 25 the usual heterogeneous crowd of that day were present, and the vast audiences, which assembled both in the forenoon, and afternoon seemed highly appreciative of the two most excellent lectures, which were given. Colville was the speaker of the morning. After answering a number of questions propounded by the audience, "Spiritualism versus Orthodoxy—Cooperation verses Competition," was taken as the subject of the discourse, and it has seldom been our privilege to listen to so profound, so complete and comprehensive a rendition. The vast audience was at once charmed, edified, and instructed.

Colville held that competition in the highest sense is productive of good. If people are competitive for the sake of being better able to help each other, then competition is praiseworthy and productive of the grandest results. Self-preservation is essential to the practice of the highest principles of fraternity. We do not teach self-immolation or self-abnegation.

Self-abnegation is a figment of fetish superstition. We advocate self-elevation and self-culture to beneficent ends. The more you know the better off you are, and the more you can teach others. You can do a great deal more good when you are strong, healthy, wise and attractive. We believe in worshipping God in the beauty of holiness. Holiness is symmetry, and to worship in the beauty of holiness is to be unfolded symmetrically in all the attributes of our being.

Humanity in its perfected state is not revealed until the humane and philanthropic is unfolded. The philosophical doctrine of error is that if you make mistakes you have to suffer for it, and thank God you have to suffer for it, for if you did not, you would go through eternity maimed, like a bird with its pinions clipped.

Spiritualism is threefold; it is scientific, philosophical and religious. It must be built on the rock of truth, not on the sliding sands of superstition.

We do not believe in a historical God or a geographical God. We believe in an eternal and infinite God—A God that is too large to be put within the covers of a book. The revelation of our God is altogether too grand to be compassed by any human idea.

No soul is lost, and there is no soul anywhere that is not eventually uplifted. The possibilities of the archangel are within you.

When you pass to the other side of life, the same as here, you will enjoy as much as you deserve, and suffer as much as you merit. No one man can make an agreement with God for your shortcomings.

Spiritualism is good to live by, but it is not good to die by. Its emphatic affirmation is; Man thou shalt never die! Its philosophy is the philosophy of eternal evolution. Its corner stone is the resurrection, the ascension and glorification of humanity.

"Is That Curl False?" was given by one in the audience as a subject for the closing poem. No one but Colville could have elucidated from such an uncanny subject such poetic imagery and such a delightful application to the social condition of the day.

The Cassadaga Lake Free Association Board met the 30th, and settled many points relative to the season of '96. Some of the best talent of the land is already secured for the platform, and the program of 96 will be virtually the promulgation and discussion of the "Natural Law of the Spiritual World," not according to Drummond, but investigated demonstrated and proven by actual experience and upon strictly scientific principles. The first Sunday of the Camp July 12th, Robert G. Ingersol is to be the speaker, and the entrance fee at the gate that day will be 50 cents.

The Leolyn House (open from May 1 to October 1) is located in a beautiful grove of twenty acres, upon the shore of "middle lake" of Cassadaga chain of lakes in Chautauqua County, New York.

The owner, Mrs. A. L. Pettengill, of Cleveland, O., has spared neither palus nor expense to make the house perfect in all its appointments, and the management wish to announce that they give their whole and attention to the comfort of their guest, they also have a library of five hundred volumes for their exclusive use. and Mrs. F. A. Smith are the managers.

The South Park House and restaurant, by N. E. Wilcox, Moore's restaurant and ice cream polar, in the Reed Cottage near the Amphitheater, Bennett's restaurant and ice cream parlor, in the Park House block, Champlain's ice cream parlor, near the gate, and a number of others, afford ample supplies for the comfort and up building of the physical man.

Robert G. Ingersoll, Sunday afternoon July 12th, without introduction or preliminaries, plunged at once into his subject, and was oblivious to everything but its vastness. The great restless, buzzing audience was at once silenced, and was, as one body, carried along on the waves of his eloquence.

He began by saying: " I too, have a religion. My religion is the religion of Liberty. What light is to the eye, what air is to the lungs, liberty is to the soul. Liberty is not a means to an end. It is an end."

But it is entirely superfluous to quote from so masterful as that of Robert G. Ingersol. The thinking, reasoning, sensible world is too familiar with his ringing words, which have electrified it from shore to shore, to need them herein transcribed.

No new propositions were given, no new inspiration as a Co-worker with the thinkers and workers of the age, who are laboring to move the world forward; and yet there was that in his presence and in his words which was uplifting, and to those who had never before heard or read him, there was a lesson never to be forgotten.

It would seem impossible that a soul so rich in all the qualities of a high, broad and useful manhood—one who is so clear a discerned, and so heroic a defender of the rights of men, women and children; one posed of such tender sympathies and emotions, such tender sympathies and emotions, such quick perception and hearty response to all that is good, true and beautiful in the material world, could so long flounder about in the dead sea of Agnosticism, without even manifesting a desire to know if there be an immortal shore beyond—a sphere where the activities and possibilities of his great and good nature may still go forward in the work to which he has devoted his life, and yet only just begun, viz.: the work of disseminating wisdom, encouraging reason, of ridding the human mind of false and belittling ideas of God and religion, and the establishing in their souls the glorious principles of liberty, justice and equality.

But Robert G. Ingersoll is nearing the other shore, and some bright day he will step out of the old body, which will no longer tenantable, into the larger and broader arena of life everlasting. No longer trammeled by bodily infirmities or material obstacles, he will go forward with a fresh impetus in his work as a reformer and liberator—the ties of family and home, of friends and co-thinkers, unbroken.

Mrs. R. S. Lillie, who is now happily a resident of this camp took her departure to-day, Thursday, for the Island Lake Mich. Camp, where she will deliver three lectures, then return home for a week, then go to the Eastern Camps until Aug. 16, the time of her engagements here. Her brief speech this morning in conference was exceedingly touching, especially to the old workers, who have followed Mrs. Lillie with their sympathy and solicitude, and worked shoulder to shoulder with her, as it were, during her sixteen years of labor in this camp.

She said she had been here since the second season of the camp, and well remembered the speakers stand covered with the rough branches of the hemlock, studded with water lilies, and hung by Mrs. Skidmore with pictures of her favorite poets. The women were the most enthusiastic workers in clearing up and making the camp the beautiful spot it is. Sisters, Skidmore, Purple, Sage, Mrs. David Ramsdell, Mrs. Cobb of Dunkirk and Mrs. Joan Carter, were among the number who burned bush and cooked good dinners for the men who did the heavier work.

Friday morning, the 17th, the Children's Progressive Lyceum gave its first public exhibition, and in view of the fact that they had only four days in which to prepare for it, it was a great success. George A. Fuller of Worcester, Mass., and Mrs. Carrie E. S. Twing of Westfield each gave the children a pleasant little talk. Miss Austin, the kindergarten teacher, had a class of her pupils present and gave a very pretty object lesson. Miss Lois Moulton of Grand Rapids, Mich., and Miss Annette Rittenhouse of New York City, Conduct the Lyceum and seem to be well equipped for the work, and are already making it very attractive. They have 40 pupils enrolled, and have formulated a systematic and progressive line of work.

There are a number of mediums on the grounds, most of them on the mental and spiritual plane. P. L. O. A. Keeler and family, including Mrs. M. W. Leslie, the mother of Mrs. Keeler, are at their cottage on Lincoln Park. Keeler has plenty to do as a slate writing and phenomena medium.

The Campbell Brothers are at their lovely home on the bluffs. As a spirit artist Allan Campbell has no superior.

There are many who are highly endowed with the gift of clairvoyances and psychometry; among them are Mrs. J. E. Allen of Elmira, located in the Sage Cottage on Cottage Row: Senior De Orvies, at the Henderson Cottage on Lincoln Park, who has formed a class in Psychometric or Soul-Teaching and is eminently qualified to instruct in lines scientific. Senior De Orvies is also giving readings and lessons in the science of Palmistry, and is much admired.

Miss Hattie Danford, late of New York, a very able psychometrist and palmist, is also giving readings and instructions at her rooms at the Hyde Cottage on 4th Street.

Banner of Light, July 25, 1896
To the Editor of the *Banner of Light:*
Hamburg, N. Y., July 15, 1896
A convention has been called of Spiritualists and Spiritualist Societies of the State of New York, to be held in the Auditorium of the Cassadaga Lake Free Association at Lily Dale, N. Y., Aug 21, 1896, for the purpose of organizing a State Association to be an auxiliary to the National Spiritualists' Association: The members of local societies to be represented in person or by delegates sent by the society—each society to have a vote for each member.

The Spiritual Education and Protective Union has its annual meeting at the above date, and proposes to turn over its affairs to the State Association when organized. Frank Fuller

There are a number of classes in the different lines of spiritual teachings, all of which are of value in their particular departments. Miss Hattie Danforth has formed a class in psychic teachings, also in palmistry, and is doing good work. Prof. B. T. Pratt of Painsville, Ohio, is instructing classes and lecturing on the subject of phrenology.

On Tuesday forenoon an able discussion upon psychometry took place at the Auditorium. Brooks, Prof. Pratt and others contributed valuable thoughts. Prof. William Lockwood, of Chicago, was the speaker, and it is our opinion that, if the brain of any one present was befogged by dogmatism and superstition, the electrifying searchlight of his reasoning must forever dispelled it.

P. L. O. A. Keeler.

The Campbell brothers:
Charles Shrouds and Allen Campbell.

Lockwood is one of the savants of the Cassadaga platform, who plants the standard of reason and investigation and yields to no man in his devotion to truth. . His philosophy rests upon foundations laid by scientific research, experiment, and investigation of many years, and contemporaneously with the most eminent thinkers of the age. He always attracts audiences of thinkers and investigators, and always gives a new impetus to the spirit of investigations.

Friday was "Lyceum Day." The exercises of the morning showed marked improvement on the part of the children. The Delsarte instruction was by Miss Rittenhouse of New York City. The elocution and spiritual teachings, which bring out the child's love of nature and the reasoning faculties, conducted jointly by Miss Rittenhouse and Miss Lou Moulton, are of a truly spiritual and educational character.

The entertainment by the Lyceum in the evening was largely attended, and the excellent program elicited continuous and enthusiastic applause.

Miss Austin, the kindergarten teacher, and her band of dear little children, have participated in the public entertainments, and added greatly to their interest and brightness.

The young people's meeting takes place this Saturday a. m. in the Auditorium. It is now regularly organized, and has a fine program for this morning. This is a step in the right direction, and the people are taking great interest in it.

Our six-week's of encampment here end to-morrow, Sunday, the 23d of August.

The record of the season is a clean one, and the Executive Board and members of the Cassadaga Lake Free Association have reason to be proud of it, and to take new courage in future action for it's extension. Our platform has been honored with some of the best thinkers and highest inspirations of the age.

The most vital questions—social, political, scientific and religious—have been discussed, with the acumen of scholarship and the intuition of the prophet and seer. And although the stringency of the times has had the effect to lessen the numbers in attendance here, as elsewhere, and the valuation of property is somewhat depreciated in con-

Swimmers on the lake.

sequence of the same, yet so far as the interest of the people is concerned, and the spiritual and intellectual status of the camp, the present season was a success. Orpha E. Hammond

Banner of Light, September 5, 1896
The Closing Saturday and Sunday At Cassadaga Camp, N.Y.
The unabated interest manifested up to the very last hour of the session of 1896 at this ideal resort is of itself a prophecy of its future success. It seemed during the last two days that every body was striving to make the very most of every precious moment of time.

At the conference hour in the a. m. questions of moment to the spiritual up building of the Camp were discussed, the speakers and thinkers of the Camp entering with earnestness and valor into the intellectual and spiritual arena, equipped with the armor of truth and practical suggestions. Mrs. R. S. Lillie occupied the lecture hour in the afternoon, and give forth valuable and exalted thoughts upon the true mission of Spiritualism.

Sunday a.m. Mrs. Jennie B. H. Jackson charmed her large audience by her characteristic simplicity and eloquence in dealing with the subjects given her by the people. She also gave improvisations.

The June 11th picnic of 1897 was well attended and one of the featured speakers, W.W. Hicks was quoted as saying: In his fervently eloquent way, that Cassadaga stands for the most important, the most divine and most highly educational movement on earth. It is the affirmative declaration of a spiritual universe, an immanent God, an established relation and communion between the two worlds— the seen and unseen—that man has never fallen, except upward. The little matter of conversing with our mother or grandmother on the other side of life is not the all-important question. The main thing is the coming in touch with the spiritual universe, and being able to commune with or without the aid of a medium. Cassadaga is a school, and everybody that comes within its gates feels the divine influence of that school. Spiritual truth is seen with the spiritual eyes. Education helps the angle over there to thunder through us. Education of right sort will not hinder, but help, the downpour of spiritual gifts.

Bro. Lyman Howe was called for, and in his calm and impressive manner said, in substance, that enough had already been said on the subject to furnish food for thought for a whole year. Our venerable brother, Dr. J. F. Carter, who has been clairvoyant, medium and healer, well known to us all, put in an earnest plea in favor of inspiration.

Mrs. Agnew said she thought while we were all seemingly disagreeing, we were agreeing in the central thought—that there were not many schools that are educating the individual but are filling them with other people's ideas. Cassadaga's mission is to educate the people to accept educated teachers.

Mrs. Myra F. Payne made an earnest plea in favor of integral education—education that draws out the inherent qualities of the soul—an education that does not exclude, but includes inspiration. Frank Walker digressed somewhat from the subject. He made a plea for the State Association and for the semi-centennial celebration forthcoming.

It is a universally accepted fact that Cassadaga's yearly programs are never surpassed as to breadth of thought and variety of talent offered and in this year 1897 we are better equipped with platform ability than at any previous time in the camp's history—as a thoughtful survey of our program will demonstrate. At no one camp or point of the compass will there be such a collection of well-known mediums and healing psychics as at Cassadaga the present season. Here the seeker after phenomena cannot fail to realize the complete gratification of his desire in this direction, nor the honest investigator goes hence with the truth undemonstrated.

P. L. O. A. Keeler, the eminent slate-writer, is located for the season at his cottage on Lake View Avenue. The Campbell Brothers, spirit artists, will welcome believer or investigator at their home on Marion Street. F. Corden White, test and business medium, who has so satisfactorily served the Association in seasons past, and in the recent purchase of a desirable property on Lake View Avenue, has become a resident of the camp, figures among the season's attractions. The Bangs Sisters of Chicago, so well known to the public, are located on Library Street, and will be until the middle of August.

Mrs. Philip Wreidt, trumpet medium of Dayton, Ohio, so favorably known to camp visitors, will occupy the old quarters at the Olmstead Cottage on Cleveland Avenue. Mrs. Maude Gillette, slate-writer and materializing medium, who has a flattering following, will, with a party of Chicago friends, be domesticated in the Henderson Cottage, Lake View Avenue. (Lake View Avenue was also called Cottage Row)

Mrs. Maggie Waite, platform test medium of California, will be located on Melrose Park, and has been engaged by the Association for the entire season. Besides this number of celebrated psychics, there are present many others of lesser note.

A leading innovation of the season of '97, and a most happy thought on the part of our indefatigable President, were the opening exercises on Friday afternoon, when the honored pioneers of this institution held at

The Bangs sisters, Elizabeth and May.

the Auditorium an informal reception, to which all our little world was invited. Music and a delightful recital of early reminiscence from a score of Cassadaga's early founders constituted the program.

In the group of interesting pioneers whose faith in man, in things visible and invisible, and in the cause of Spiritualism inspiring and sustaining them in the work of building the foundations of this prosperous and permanent institution, was for many years the St. Peter at our gate—Dr. Jeremiah Carter—who twenty years ago heard the spirit voices bidding him to go to Cassadaga and start the movement that has developed into the leading Spiritualistic camp in the world.

Thomas Grimshaw, a young English Spiritualist, a growing man intellectually, and a favorite wherever known and heard, lectured as Robert Ingersol never can unless touched by the divine spirit of inspiration, on "A Chapter in the Experiences of a Human Soul." A deeply scientific discourse, awakening hearty applause and great praise, to the extent of being pronounced by able critics to be one of the finest addresses ever delivered on our platform.

Tuesday afternoon witnessed a meeting of the dreamy orient and the matter-of-fact occident at Cassadaga. A. H. Dharmapala, the distinguished son of the orient, and representative of an ideal philosophy, with his lofty views on the brotherhood of man, his simple and severe habits of life, his mild and sweetly spiritual face, modest, diffident manners and soft, gentle voice, and picturesque figure clothed in his native garb of flowing orange robes, completely captured an audience who through the years have welcomed men and women of all shades and beliefs.

Wednesday there was a union service participated in by a number of our speakers. W. C. Hodge, of Chicago, a pioneer worker in Spiritualism, led the service in a clean cut twenty minutes' talk; Said he: Truth has many sides; each separate religion extant has some truth—as much as its people can comprehend, for there must be on the part of the recipient the ability to receive.

Spiritualism is a natural thing; to me naturalism would be the more proper term. As Spiritualist we have gotten rid of a belief in the supernatural. We have unfolded and come out into the light naturally as the flowers bloom.

The other life is just as natural as this, and is no great distance away. As Harriet Beecher Stowe said: "It lies around us like a cloud." We are absolutely in the spirit-world now, and it is the privilege of every one to so live that he can be in constant rapport with this other world. I know this is absolutely true, for in the last twenty years there has not been a single day that I have not been perfectly conscious of this world of spirit.

Isn't it a little curious that the so-called heathen, for whom the church and missionaries have raised millions of dollars to convert to the Christian religion, are coming over here on our side of the water to teach this nation good morals and a higher spirituality of life?

Spiritualism—like any other religion must be judged by its fruits. Religion is practical righteousness, or it isn't anything, for it isn't what we believe, but what we do.

Every day we are taking psychological impress from spirits, and it is our duty to see that right and justice is done in this world, so that the spirits who go out may be of a higher class individually, for these spirits that go out undeveloped are paupers, and often worse.

Thomas Grimshaw followed with some practical thoughts on Spiritualism, urging that we cease living in the past, for Spiritualists spend too much time fighting creeds that we have been told are dead, or dying. It is time to wage war against living wrongs.

On the morning of August 7, at his cottage on Caldwell Park, the immortal spirit of the venerable and universally respected Jeremiah Carter went to join the great majority of whose existence and presence he was daily conscious.

It was to Carter the voices spoke prophetically in 1877 of the Cassadaga that was to evolve out of the pioneer movement he was bidden to start. And it was "Uncle Jerry's" faith in the wisdom and guidance of these divine messengers that prompted and inspired him in the initiatory steps that have resulted in the fulfillment of all and even more than was promised. It seems, indeed, a fitting finale that he should lay aside the frail mortal (for he was eighty-four, and very feeble) at beautiful Lily Dale he loved so well, and that his transition should be swift and peaceful like the falling into slumber of a weary child.

The sudden announcement that the angel of death had visited the camp and borne its aged founder across the mystic river, caused no gloom, but rather rejoicing in the knowledge that all was well with the newly born soul in the spirit realm, where was prepared for him a mansion, the building of which he had accomplished by his mortal life of unswerving devotion to duty, uprightness, purity and brotherly love. His sons took the remains to Fredonia, N. Y., for internment by the side of his companion and wife.

A leading social event of the last week of camp was a Mediums Reception on Thursday evening at the Auditorium—a delightfully informal and pleasant affair—attended by most of the campers and all of the leading media. The entertainment consisted of presentations by mediums and short addresses from several of them, with music interspersed. Our honored President being called for, he felicitously responded "Our mediums, what would we do without them: they are the salt of the earth, the foundation of our cause, and the central magnet of our camp, for we first demonstrate, then spin fine theories. Since the early commencement of my work at Cassadaga I have recognized the very important part that mediumship takes in the promulgation of the cause for which we as an association are organized, and one of my first efforts after becoming a trustee, was to equip, at my own expense, the camp with more mediums. I have always been the friend of true mediums, and no genuine psychic ever left these grounds feeling other than friendly toward me. During all these years I have always encouraged the attendance of mediums at our camp, and I assure you it affords me encouragement and satisfaction to be able to say that Cassadaga leads all other camps as to the superiority and number of first-class mediums yearly in attendance, and in this season of 1897 we are surpassing even ourselves. Again, in the name of our cause and camp, I welcome these mediums who are the binding links between the spiritual and physical world, the chosen messengers between the visible and the invisible."

During the week just closed the brilliant and illustrious Annie Besant, "high priestess of Theosophy" and her co-worker, the Countess Wachtmeister, accompanied by Miss Wilson, Librarian of the London Theosophical Society, have entertained and delighted Cassadagans with three public addresses and as many parlor talks. Mrs. Besant, who is an English woman, is of medium height, inclining toward the embonpoint, possessing a strong, intellectual face, bright, expressive eyes, a well-modulated voice, a rare smile, that frequently illuminates the face—in short, hers is a strongly magnetic, striking personality.

The first address of this lady was delivered Tuesday evening, Aug 17, on "Theosophy and Its Teachings." Theosophy she defined as Divine Wisdom, dealing with the deeper sides of life; with the nature of man and his relations to the universe; teaching how he may come in touch with different worlds, and utilize this knowledge beneficially. Theosophy teaches that man is a living, spiritual intelligence, and a soul that possesses a body, rather than a body with a soul. After physical dissolution his spiritual nature continues to live, and it is this spiritual side of man that gives him his special individual characteristics.

Banner of Light, September 18, 1897

Six weeks waxed and waned since the opening of the season 1897 at Camp Cassadaga, six full and complete weeks, into which have been crowded much of profit, benefit and enjoyment, that nevermore will effaced from fair memory's page of fade less pictures. And now the chapter has closed, the drama been enacted, the music ceased its harmonious pulsation's, the lights are out, and the large crowds of summer guests departed, only a few of the multitude still lingering to enjoy nature's beauty and solitude.

From every point of view the season was a successful one, and the management expresses itself satisfied with the attendance and financial results, both being an encouraging improvement over last year, and a decidedly hopeful outlook for the future.

Continuous rainy, cool weather depleted to some extent to crowds of Sunday excursionists, but this shrinkage was more than over-balanced by the permanent attendance of those from remote distances, a large percentage of whom were newcomers at Cassadaga.

It was universally conceded by the able critics that the program of '97 exceeded in brilliancy and variety of talent any of its predecessors. Most of the old favorites were retained while several new stars were added to the collection, winning the plaudits of audiences. Even at this early date there are reliable indications that a still larger amount of new talent will appear in the galaxy of next year's bright lights.

Great credit is due our mediums, of whom there were fifty present, for their part in making the season a complete success, and for the magnificent work accomplished by and through them in the way of demonstrating to the investigator the continuity of life. An evident desire for knowledge along the higher lines of spiritual unfoldment was manifest in the large attendance at the various classes in sessions.

Mental science was taught by Francis E. Mason; Oriental philosophy by Dr. W. W. Hicks; spiritual unfoldment by Mrs. Cora L. V. Richmond; Buddhism, by its representative, A. H. Dharmapala; Phrenology and psychology, by J. Clegg Wright; and a variety of other interesting things, such as hypnotism, astrology, palmistry, music and dancing.

The Children's Progressive Lyceum under the capable leadership of Miss Annette Rittenhouse, gave a series of public entertainment's, suggestive of their mental drill and Delsarte exercises, which occupied their morning hours, terminating in an excursion around the lakes.

The Young People's Literary Society—organized last year by George H. Brooks, and still chaperoned by him—was delightfully active in receptions and other social functions. It is the very laudable purpose of this Society to raise funds for the erection of a building of their own, which shall contain gymnasium, reading room, public parlors and dining hall. Their first move in this direction was a tennis court and croquet grounds on the lakefront, over which they presided with grace and skill.

The morning conferences lost none of their old-time attractiveness, rather gaining in this respect.

The Thought Exchange continued to be an attractive as well as educational center, while the forest meetings, formerly designated pow-wows, have become a valuable auxiliary to the Association work, evolving into quiet, orderly gatherings that would be a credit to any place and any people.

The music rendered during the season was of superior

order. The Northwestern Band and Orchestra, one of Cassadaga's leading attractions, received many justly merited encomiums; while Douglas Lane, the sweet baritone soloist, captured the camp with his artistic singing constantly growing in favor in favor as the days increased. There is a strong desire expressed for the employment of Lane and his Male Quartet for next year, which we trust our gracious trustees will favorably consider as they do their people's known wishes.

During the closing week Mrs. Carrie E. S. Twing, Mrs. A. E. Sheets and Hon. A. B. Richmond provided the intellectual food, to the delectation of the crowd and interest that did not decline until the close of the session.

Sunday evening, Aug. 29, the closing event of the season was a large and enthusiastic love feast, held in the Auditorium, the love feast of wondrous spiritual harmony, good fellowship, loving appreciation and bright prophecy for the future success and growth of our Zion—beautiful Cassadaga.

Many leading speakers and mediums, and some visitors from a distance, spoke charmingly of our camp and its prospects. All vied with each other in their commendation of the season's program, and the noble work of the management, uttering glowing prophecies for the future, and assurances of the loyal support and conference of the mediums and speakers, all of which was very gratifying to the management and trustees present and, combined with the universal good-will and faith expressed from all sides, has left with our noble management a feeling of hopefulness, unsurpassed in former years.

There were receptions and benefits galore at Cassadaga during the season. The last one, occurring after the close of the regular session, was tendered our popular Chairman, George H. Brooks, who, during his two years' service at this camp, has grown and improved in many ways, gaining a strong hold upon the affections of the people, for none can fail to be won by his genial, whole souled ever pleasant and cordial manner. In short, Brooks has proven a valuable adjunct to the camp, and we predict that he will be invited to preside the coming year of 1898.

At the recent reorganization of the Board of Trustees the following persons were unanimously reelected officers for the coming year: A. Gaston, President; T. J. Skidmore, Treasurer; A. E. Gaston, Secretary; Miss Kate O. Peate, Corresponding Secretary.

"The Cassadagan," banner of the Cassadaga Lake Free Association, will this year be edited by our new trustee, F. G. Neelin, Seaforth, Ont. Neelin is an editor, a gentleman of intellectual and business ability, who enters upon his new duties as a trustee with a lofty purpose and hearty earnestness that bespeaks his valuables as a co-worker and we prophesy that our little paper will lose none of its merits under his capable management. The paper will be double its former size, issued monthly, for fifty cents per year. It will contain all important camp and Association news, beside a large amount of original matter from first class contributors, and we believe will generously patronized by friends and lovers of Cassadaga.

It is a fact worthy of comment that departing guests were unanimous in their protestations of enjoyment of pleasures experienced during their sojourn at the camp, and their avowed intent to return next season accompanied by friends.

As previously stated, there was a larger percentage of new-comers this season than usual, several of whom invested in real estate, while others are contemplating a purchase—real estate being more in demand at present than for some few years past.

Early in September Dr. W. W. Hicks will open on the grounds a School of Philosophy of Intelligence; good accommodations can be secured for those wishing to attend. For terms Address the doctor at Lily Dale, N. Y. All is well that ends well.—Shirley Belle

Banner of Light, March 12, 1898

Buffalo—J. W. Dennis writes; our camps in this state number four. First, Lily Dale, at Cassadaga, which has been the camp of the nation, when we had but three or four camps in the country; but now that we have over sixty camps in the United States, it has become one of the many good ones, and its glory has somewhat departed. In the days when H. D. Barrett, your worthy editor, was a presiding officer there, and five thousand people were often seen on her beautiful grounds, Lily Dale was in its glory; but the lasting good that Lily Dale Camp has done can never be forgotten by our Spiritualists while time shall last. Findley's Lake, a few miles south of Cassadaga in Chautauqua county, is not called a camp because it lacks the needed organization; yet I am told that fifteen hundred people often gather there to hear some of our best speakers, and there is a prospect that one of these days it may become a regular camp, after the style of our other camps.

Lake George Camp is in a good healthy condition, and will hold the regular annual meetings in August 1898. There is a good and regularly organized camp at Freeville, Tompkins County, which is in a healthy condition, well officered and well located. It is about thirty miles south of Auburn, N. Y., and on the line of the Lehigh Valley railroad. Your correspondent was one of the organizers of this good camp. Bro. B. L. Robinson, M. D., is President and resides at McLean, Tompkins County, N.Y.

There is a new camp on Oneida Lake that came into existence last season and its circulars claim that there will be a camp meeting held there all of the month of August, 1898. Bro. G. W. Kates is President, and resides in Rochester, N. Y. This camp has a fine location and your correspondent had a hand in organizing this camp also.

There is room for camps in all parts of our State, and we sadly need a Buffalo Camp, which would strictly be a Buffalo camp, and we may have one yet, when people get wakened up to the fact that there are a score of good locations just at our doors, on the Niagara river, that flows past our beautiful city, the Queen of the West.

Banner of Light, May 21, 1898

W. H. Bach has built an elegant pagoda to the north of the Auditorium, where his wife Evelena dispenses literature, badges, taffy, patriotism, sorrowful to relate, the cigar nuisance! His idea is that some one will supply them, so long as there is a demand, and that he does not add to the sum of smokers by dealing them out to those who want them. The cigar spot is the only blemish on this beautiful and tastefully arranged pagoda. Lily Dale welcomes all varieties of people, and tolerates all their creeds and fads without endorsing any. Spiritualism first, last and all the time is the inspiration that has created these beautiful grounds, and sus-

The Pagoda.

tains these annual feasts with the best platform talent to be found in the land and the most reliable and wonderful phases of mediumship, presenting phenomenon that defy criticism and meet the demand of scientific demonstration.

F. Cordon White, P. L. O. A. Keeler, The Campbell Brothers, Mrs. Moss, Coles, The Bangs Sisters, Mrs. Wriedt, Mrs. O'Donnell, Maggie Waite, Maggie Turner, Isa Wilson Kaynor, and Mrs. Hartwell, Henry B. Allen, besides astrologers, palmists, theosophists etc, afford a variety to suit all tastes; and every day new wonders are reported by investigators.

The grounds are more beautiful than ever. The Leolyn, outside the grounds, has added much to the attractiveness around the gate. All appointments are tasteful, and Beauty reigns queen of Lily Dale. The Campbell Brothers have built a new cottage on the buff next to the gate, and made a veritable paradise of the spot.

Everything points to 1898 as the banner year of the Camp in many respects. The Pettibones are giving satisfactory séances, and from those who attest I have heard most flattering accounts of the "proof palpable" of immortality that are given in their séances. Maggie Waite dispenses the "platform tests" to the delight of many and surprise of many others. We are looking forward to a greeting from the sunny face and earnest soul of Harrison D. Barrett, who is to adorn the platform soon.—Lyman C. Howe

Banner of Light, July 2, 1898

We have had many letters of inquiry in relation to Cassadaga Camp at Lily Dale, N. Y., and would state to our numerous friends, through the columns of your valuable paper, that there is not the slightest truth or foundation in the report of a fire having destroyed part of the buildings. There has never been one building destroyed by fire or accident since the camp's formation eighteen years since.

We have just held the annual picnic of three days on June 17, 18, 19, with marked success, as in former years, and people who have been accustomed to attending the gatherings were seen, with the addition of many new faces, some coming hundreds and thousands of miles to participate in the pleasures that are here found. This is the eighteenth annual celebration of this picnic, which is only a forerunner of a long and instructive round of pleasure, for the season of this beautiful camp, which opens Friday, July 15 and continues until August 28.

Sunday afternoon there was an exhibition of spirit portraits obtained through the mediumship of the Campbell Brothers, at their new cottage at the entrance to the grounds. Hundreds viewed these works, and fully appreciated them.

Sunday night a reception was given at the Grand Hotel in which many speakers and mediums took part. Taking it all together, the June picnic of '98 was a grand success, for people all over the country are beginning to realize that this is an ideal spot, and by the numbers that have already taken up their quarters here for the summer season, one can readily see that this beautiful place is becoming more and more popular every season. This season the management has presented one of the finest programs possible to procure from the lecture field. There will also be an array of the finest physical mediums in the United States, embracing all phases of the phenomena; many physical mediums are already here, and numbers are arriving to stay throughout the season.

The improvements on the grounds are still in progress, and will delight the eye of the visitor. The Grand Hotel looks refreshing with its new decorations, and is now open for the reception of guests. The Hotel Leolyn is also open for guests, and has many improvements and beautiful surroundings.

The camp at Lily Dale has never looked more beautiful, and all outside troubles are forgotten in this charming resort on the lakes, where one can come and say, "I feel at peace with all the world." Programs for the season of '98 can be had on application to the Secretary, Lily Dale, New York.—Campbell Brothers

Banner of Light, July 9, 1898

Most camps charge ten cents a day as a ground fee. Cassadaga charges fifteen cents admission and ten cents a day afterwards, or $3.50 for a season ticket covering the entire forty-five days of camp. Board and room can be had at all prices, but during the season it averages about $1 a day, unless you go to the high priced hotels when it ranges from $7 to $12 per week.

But to those who wish an outing at the lowest price, the proper thing to do is to secure a room at from $1 to

The Leolyn Hotel.

$1.50 per day which two people can occupy, bring an oil stove with you, a few dishes and keep house yourself. You need not to be afraid you will be considered small or stingy, as you will have plenty of company.

There are two grocery stores on the grounds, which carry a complete stock of goods especially adapted to campers' use, two bakeries and restaurants where regular meals can be had at 25 cents each. All lectures, conferences, and thought exchanges are free, not even a collection being taken at any of them.

Not to be outdone by the rest, your humble servant has also improved, and visitors to the camp, will see the result of it in a neat Chinese Pagoda, tastefully ornamented and painted, occupying a prominent place in the center of the park, between the Auditorium and the Grand Hotel, where a complete stock of Spiritualistic free thought, astrological, theosophical and other books can be found, also the Spiritualistic papers and an opportunity for leaving your subscription for the same; also souvenirs of the camp will be for sale.—W. H. Bach

The Sunflower, August 1898 (first issue; William Bach, owner and editor)

Col. R. T. Van Horn, for forty years editor and proprietor of the *Kansas City Journal* and Congressman from Missouri for a number of years, is spending a few days at Lily Dale.

The Campbell Brothers have a most attractive spot in their picture gallery located in their new home near the entrance. Pierre L. O. A. Keeler, well known to the public for twenty years as an independent slate-writing medium, announces a book giving full instructions for home development. While talking of pictures, it will be well to remember the Bangs Sisters. We are informed that they are producing an average of three pictures daily.

And E. W. Wallis will arrive this evening; and Mrs. Chiswell are expected, and the local Y. P. S. U. will give them a real English tea at the residence of Skidmore. The above come from England as members of the Y. P. S. U. and as such will be gladly welcomed at Lily Dale. Wallis is editor of *The Two Worlds*.

Light of Truth, June 24, 1899

    Hon. A. Gaston was active and happy. And why should he not be? Having received the endorsement of the people by being elected to the congress of the United States (Meadville, Pennsylvania) in a district that is normally opposed to his party views, and with a full knowledge of his attitude as a Spiritualist, he still represents the C. L. F. A. as its honored president, and this annual picnic surpasses all antecedents as a financial success. It is the first time that these meetings have paid all expenses and left a surplus in the treasury. The gate receipts were $6 more than last year, the collections on the ground were $5 over last year, and the Saturday evening dance had 41 couples as against 27 last year. Undertones of discontent are always in the air. Enough of censorious criticism, and personal prejudice is always on exhibition to ventilate unhealthy spleen and furnish a measly diet for all who thrive best on such pabulum, while there is an abundance of wholesome nourishment for souls that aspire to the good and true, and cherish kindness and toleration toward those whose instincts impel them to evil and lead them into trouble.—Lyman C. Howe

Banner of Light, August 4, 1899

    Camp Cassadaga is booming. If all camps for the promulgation of Spiritualism are as active as is Cassadaga, there will be a work done this season, which will advance the cause and achieve much lasting good. This platform has never sent out greater truths or brighter gems of thought than have been uttered therein this season during these first two weeks. The attendance on the grounds is double that of last year or the past five years at this early stage of the meeting. Mrs. Lease, J. Clegg Wright, Lyman C. Howe, A. B. Richmond and Mrs. Agnew are the notable speakers present, with many other new aspirants who are coming into work. Conferences, thought exchange and Forest Temple meetings are all under way and highly interesting. Mediums are kept busy, and everything points to a lively interest and investigation into the truth of spirit-return and continuity of life.

    Canada is sending over large delegations, and we are glad to announce the coming of Rev. Dr. Austin, who was recently on trail for heresy. He will speak Aug. 25 and 27.

    The restaurants are kept in fine order. The hotels are

The Forest Temple.

full and well conducted. The dances are, as they have ever been, orderly and first class. Then there is the bowling alley, always clean and attractive, and last but not least, the far famed Northwestern Band filling the groves with music.—L. B. B.

Light of Truth, September 30, 1899

Editor Bach of the *Sunflower* has bought the "Chase" Cottage at 17 South Street, Lily Dale and moved his printing and publishing plant into it, making the needed changes in rooms etc.

Cassadagan, December 1899

Arrangement for the school of Science and Philosophy to be held in Lily Dale in the coming camp season have been made and the terms are here announced. The school will be conducted by J. Clegg Wright, and will be five sections namely: (1) Physiology (2) Mental Science (3) Mediumship (4) Philosophy-Ancient and Modern (5) Myths—Ancient and Modern. Wright proposes to charge the reasonable sum of $5 for the whole course and $1 for a course of five lectures. It is intended that each lecture shall be printed and sent out. We hope that this may prove a help to those seeking light and knowledge.

Cassadagan, March 1900

On Feb. 13, 1900 the icemen were scraping snow and water from the ice, when it broke and a beautiful span of horses went down to their death. They would have been rescued but for a heavy iron scraper held them down. (The horses were being used for "ice farming" a common industry on the lakes of Western New York.)

Banner of Light, May 26, 1900

Season of 1900

The management of beautiful Lily Dale is preparing for a great time this coming season. Every one seems to be entering into the spirit of making everything attractive for the prospective visitors, and by the way things are looking, and the number of people already on the grounds, this promises to be a banner season for this place.

Ice farming.

Unloading cargo near the beach.

Old Train Depot and first Iroquois Hotel. Leolyn Hotel with new water tank in rear across lake.

Melrose Park, 1890s.

Visitors are arriving on every train, cottages are being opened, painters and paperhangers are reaping a harvest, and many improvements are taking place all over the grounds. The Grand Hotel will soon be opened. The Leolyn Hotel, on the outside of the grounds, will open June 1. The South Park is open with quite a number of visitors on its register. All the hotels have been greatly improved.

The philosophy will be represented by a very able body of lecturers and teachers. Moses Hull, that renowned lecturer and scholar, ably assisted by his wife and a corps of the best of teachers, opened their Spiritualistic Training School on the Lily Dale Camp Grounds, May 14 and will close the same July 13. The object of the school is to train its students for public work and mediumship. The school should meet with success. A very interesting circular is published, giving details of the work. Parties interested should send to Moses Hull, Lily Dale, New York, for circulars. Many are arriving daily to attend the school.

All phases of the phenomena will be represented, and many of the finest psychic from the north, east, south and west have already rented cottages for the approaching season. Materialization, etherializations, transfiguration, etc., slate writers, spirit artists, clairvoyance, business mediums, healers, doctors, palmists, spirit photographers, trumpet mediums, and various others, will be represented. Taking all in all, what with our teachers in philosophy, and our demonstrators of the phenomena, it should insure a big season for glorious Lily Dale.

We should also mention that this place is becoming famous as a health resort. Why should it not? We have the finest drinking water, invigorating pine groves, natural lakes, situated eight hundred feet above Lake Erie, and last though not least, are the pleasant drives surrounding this locality, in fact we have every thing to make life beautiful and healthful.

We will take great pleasure in sending each applicant a fine souvenir and program upon the receipt of a two-cent stamp. Address; Campbell Brothers, Lily Dale

The Sunflower, August 15, 1900

Anna Shaw was the speaker for Sunday afternoon: There was not a seat to be had in the large auditorium. Many of

Maplewood Hotel, 1900.

Maplewood Hotel.

Maplewood Hotel.

Maplewood Hotel.

Lily Dale Lake and generating plant, 1910s.

the prominent workers in the woman's movement have been at Lily Dale on these occasions. A tent known as the "Women's Tent" is always erected on the lot just south of the T. J. Skidmore Cottage. This tent was a center of attraction. Banners with a star representing the states that have adopted woman's suffrage were planted in or near it and one of the most popular views of the ground is a picture of this tent with Mrs. Skidmore holding up the banner with two stars for Wyoming and Colorado while Mrs. A. L. Pettengill and Susan B. Anthony are seated near.

Cassadagan, September 1900

An Outing at Lily Dale

By E. F. Rugg

On August the 18th, F. M. Nichols and wife, A. G. Neeley and wife, together with the writer, embarked on the train at Bliss with no prearranged understanding of meeting, and proceeding to the far famed resort for the spiritual inclined, at Lily Dale.

Changing cars at Ashford, again at Salamanca, Jamestown and Falconer, we arrived at Lily Dale, 13 miles south of Dunkirk, 7 1/2 from Fredonia. And as first impressions are best and lasting, I am inclined to believe that our first visit to this beautiful cozy nook in the midst of lakes and dales will ever be memorable. I have been taught from infancy that Spiritualists were composed of longhaired men and short haired women who wore a No. 7 shoe, and carried the marks imbecility in their countenance, with cloven foot, seven horns, and forked tongue and all the adornments that embellish his "Satan's Majesty" pictured by Dante and St. John.

But what was our surprise on stepping from the train at Lily Dale, to be met by at least 200 of the brightest, most intelligent, fairest looking, best dressed people of the United States. As I subsequently learned, they were the elite of the whole continent and judge our surprise at meeting such an array of brilliancy with outstretched hand to welcome the stranger to their midst. The thought arose, was it our money? No, it was the essence of the association, that all pervading spirit of the true believer in Spiritualism.

We found a miniature city in the distance, surrounded by lakes upon which steamers ply to and fro, and upon 15

DAV&P Railroad.

cents depends your entrance into the Spiritual enclosure. There you find displayed the beauties of architecture, innocent amusements, flowers in profusion, shady walks, a refreshing breeze from the lake, boats rides, etc.

C. L. F. A. is written over the gate meaning Cassadaga Lake Free Association, by which they are known, represents as we are told, the trials and troubles, push, pluck, and perseverance of the promoters. Taking a primeval forest, lowland adjoining lake, draining, filling in with gravel, piling brush—much of it done by the women, showing the earnest desire for the uplifting of humanity and the dissemination of knowledge to those that have the price. I was informed upon good authority that there is at present $500,000 invested in the camp at Lily Dale.

Lily Dale is really an island. Then imagine that it was a primeval forest and then see it as it is today, one cannot help but approve and applaud the efforts and zeal of the men and women who pioneered this great resort as a camp for the belief they had in the Cause for which the camp is noted. Inside the grounds today are about 300 cottages, 2 hotels, a library and reading room, a spacious auditorium, bandstand, billiard hall, bowling alley. We found also speakers engaged for the season, polished orators, bright and witty, divided on some question, ever alert, very aggressive when the truth and sincerity were questioned, having at heart the welfare and spiritual up building of all whom they come in contact.

We met the venerable Skidmore, originator of the association, who reminds me of James Rafferty of Java, also the Hon A. Gaston, Member of Congress from Meadville, Pa., president of the association; also F. G. Neelin of Seaforth, Ontario, editor of the Cassadagan; all men of sterling worth and exceptional ability. A great feature of this camp is the ardor with which every one enters into the different amusements provided and there is always something on hand, suited for every taste and desire; and the amount of knowledge that can be acquired from the very best lectures to be obtained, is sufficient food to inwardly digest for a long time. Here is a school, which runs two months, whose main object is in the instruction to those who will hereafter devote themselves to the cause. We failed to acquire sufficient knowledge of this department of education to give impressions, but observed that it receives a very large support. Strolling about the grounds one is confronted by numerous signs before the doors such as:

Bangs Sisters, phenomenal mediums, Spirit Portraits a specialty.

Campbell Brothers—Celebrated Psychics—Slate Writing—Spirit Portraits.

Clairvoyants, and Séances; others palmists, Astrologers, test mediums, trance and healing mediums, magnetic healers, etc. The art galleries of the Bangs Sisters and the Campbell Brothers are simply beautiful beyond description. The art of these mediums in producing "Spirit Portraits" is phenomenal. One sits with the portrait of a deceased friend in their pocket, and within thirty minutes the pictures is transferred on canvas before their eyes. First comes the outline then gradually the picture develops. If you say the eyes are too light, they will change to the required color. The Bangs Sisters told the writer that under certain conditions they could get a "Spirit Portrait" of a person in "spirit Life," that never had a likeness taken, by the sitter holding the looks of their friend in their mind. However, the imagination must apply much to make a natural picture. Also one sitting for their own picture will have three to fourteen spirit friends on the background of photo. Letter writing and slate writing are also a phenomena; it is evident that some agency is employed other than the slight of hand. By placing a gold watch on one corner of the slate, the writing will be done in gold, or using a silver dollar, the same, the writing will be in silver letters.

Banner of Light, December 1, 1900

The camp season comes and goes and the few families who remain on the grounds, about sixty in number, enjoy a quiet fall and then house up for the winter. There are no churches into which they can wander and simulate their minds with another's thought, but at all times of the year, on Wednesday and Sunday evenings, the home of Dr. and Mrs. E. C. Hyde is opened to friends and strangers alike, for the exchange of ideas relative to the betterment of self and humanity.

For years Mrs. Hyde has held these classes for the purpose of awakening in the minds of all who came within their compass a realization of the fact that they are not mere puppets in the hands of circumstance or fate, but absolute masters of their destiny, masters of their own minds, and their own bodies.

The Sunflower, January 1, 1901

A long expected baptism of fire finally arrived. Friday morning December 28, at about 4:30 the people were awakened by hearing gunshots and a woman screaming and rushed to find the air lurid with the light of a fire.

When the residents arrived on the scene, the fire had so much of a start that it was useless to think of saving either of the cottages which were then afire and what goods were in the lower part were hastily removed and efforts made to prevent the further spread of the flames. C. B. Turner immediately placed two horses at the disposal of the people and one mounted by Clayton McCarthy went in one direction while another ridden by J. F. Witherall went over by Cassadaga and around Burnham giving the alarm that "Lily Dale was burning."

The news spread like wildfire and teams were hastily hitched and in an incredibly short space of time, they poured into the gates loaded with men. By this time three cottages were burning fiercely and the prospects of saving any of the center of camp looked exceedingly dubious. With the arrival of assistance four squads of workers were arranged. One party went to work on the Scheu cottage on the corner of First Avenue and Cleveland, one on the cottage at the rear of the burning ones, one on the cottages across the street from the fire and the fourth decided to tear down a cottage and thus stop the flames spreading towards the East.

All worked with a will. A bucket brigade was organized, the women pumping water and carrying it equally as well as the men. Carpets, comforters and everything that would hold water was placed over the exposed portions of the buildings and while some carried water, others stood on the roofs and verandahs and kept the cloths wet, thus stopping the spread of the flames. Two teams were procured and holes were cut into the Wadsworth cottage (#12 1st), log chains attached and soon the building was drawn to one side partly torn down and snow shoveled upon the side toward the fire. Even after this, it caught fire and had to be extinguished with snow and water.

The Lily Dale fire of 1900.

In the meantime the fire continued to spread. It started in the northwest corner of Mrs. May Colville's cottage at 7 First Avenue. From there it spread to Mrs. Nellie Warren's (#5 1st) then to the Scheu cottage at #3 First Avenue. No one supposed that the corner cottage could be saved as there was but four feet space between the two buildings. But the peculiar construction of the burned building and the use of an unlimited supply of water that ran down the street from the snow melted by the heat and the Herculean efforts of some thirty men, it was done. Large carpets were drawn over the side between the burning building and the other, ladders were raised and pails of water were poured over the peak of the roof and run down keeping the carpets and the side of the house wet. Large ladders were placed against the sides of the burning building and as the fire burned off the supports the wall was pushed away and the danger of the West was over.

On the East the fire spread to Miss Russell's cottage (#8 1st) then to the Hearn cottage (#10 1st) and photograph gallery where it was checked by the removal of the Wadsworth cottage (#12 1st).

All interest now centered on the north. There, a row of cottages, only ten or fifteen feet away, had been exposed to the heat of five burning buildings. Fortunately there were a number of small buildings, sheds and such alike, most of them low, that could be torn down or rolled away. Then the fact most of the backs of these cottages were lean-tos made it possible to put carpets on them, which were kept wet. The wood was charred so badly in many places that a finger could be pushed through it, and they caught fire a number of times, even burning good sized holes in the sides, yet the flames were successfully fought; but it had not been for the fact of Dr. Hyde's cottages contained a thirty barrel cistern full of water this row would surly have gone. As near as can be ascertained the loses are as follows: Mrs. Scheu one cottage burned, insurance $500. One cottage damaged, loss on house and furniture, $700, insurance $1,000... E. C. William's, loss on furniture, $800... Nellie Warren loss between $800 and $1,000 no insurance... Mrs. Colville loss $1,000 insurance $400... Miss Russell loss about $800 supposed to be fully insured... The Hearn cottage and photograph gallery loss about

$500- no insurance...The Wadsworth cottage $150 no insurance. The damages to the other cottages will aggregate about $700 thus making a total loss of about $6,450. As most of the people are away, the figures cannot be given accurately, but the above is a very accurate estimate.

Mrs. J. H. Turner of The Sunflower Office was one of the bravest of the "fire Ladies." She did what few men could do: went up a ladder carrying a pail of water in each hand. J. H. Turner had his hand quite badly burned by coming in contact with the house, which were fully feet from the fire. This shows how hot the fire was. He became exhausted from being overheated. Fay Johnson was partially overcome by smoke while trying to save some furniture.

General items

When E. C. Williams was awakened, he fired his pistol, which awakened many people. J. F. Witherell lost his gold watch but was fortunate enough to find it again. A. Bowers was sick abed and but two houses between his home and the fire (#5 2nd) Arrangements had been made to care for him in case it was necessary.

Graham Turner and Fred Spencer had their hands hurt slightly while at work. An engine was gotten in readiness by the Jamestown Fire Department to send up to our aid had it been necessary. Fortunately it was not, but we appreciate the kindness of our Jamestown neighbors, just as much as though they had come. It snowed slightly all thorough the fire and there was scarcely a breath of air stirring. What little there was came from the west. Nellie Warren, who is at Tallapoosa, Ga., Miss Russell, who is in Pennsylvania were notified at once.

The cottage owners of Lily Dale owe a debt of gratitude to the people of Cassadaga who responded to our call for help. Had it not been for them, few cottages would have been left standing. There are so many who are incapacitated from work among the population that our effective force numbers only about twenty men, utterly inadequate to cope with such a fire. The Cassadaga people worked with a will and it is to their efforts to a great extent that we owe the comparatively light loss.

Mrs. Louisa Scheu wishes to express her personal thanks to the heroic efforts that were made to save her corner cottage. The women deserve the greatest praise for their actions from beginning to end. While most of the men came empty handed, nearly every woman brought a pail of water with her or carpets or something to fight fire with. Lily Dale has always been a woman's right place, and when it comes to fire she fills her place to perfection.

Adelbert Robinson and Ross Spencer had the hottest station at the fire. They were on a verandah across from the Hearn cottage and gallery. Had it not been for a canvass screen that was wet and placed between them and the fire, they could hardly have retained their position. As it was, their faces were burned and Robinson's trousers were so badly scorched that they fell to pieces. Several declined to go to this point say they could not stand it. One man said to them; "It all depends on you boys." Which was true for if that building had caught fire a large three story building would have been the next to go and a dozen other houses would have gone with it.

Riley Johnson nailed up the cottages that were broken open or burned so as to require it. The origin of the fire is a mystery and no blame can be attached to anyone. The insurance men say it was a remarkable feat putting it out. Many villages with good fire departments could not have done it. The alarm was given at about 4:30 and in less than two hours five cottages had been burned, one torn down and the fire was under control.

The Sunflower, January 15, 1901

Since the fire matters have settled down at Lily Dale, the excitement consists in guessing how much would have been burned if the wind had blown hard or if we had not had so much help, or what we would have done if the water supply had given out and being thankful that it was not any worse, but a screech owl in the woods or a shrill of any kind is enough to start out a bucket brigade without waiting for any thing further.

Now the people are deep in the mysteries of fire apparatus. Some want an engine with a thousand or two feet of hose, with steam kept up at all time. Others want an arrangement whereby the association engine will be cared for all the time and in readiness to have the steam made up in a few minutes at any time. Others are anxious to see an apparatus that can be worked by hand, purchased and installed, and so the matter goes. As it stands at present the prospects look exceedingly good for the purchase of something we can pay for now, with the intention to purchase something better as soon as possible. A pump with a small supply of hose has been ordered and will be tested and if satisfactory it will be installed and more hose purchased to aid in fighting any incipient blaze.

In this connection *The Sunflower* wishes to say a word. It is not justice that the people of Lily Dale should bear the entire burden of this protection. They will organize a company and care for things, but every property owner should aid to the extent of his interest and ability in securing such apparatus as will render us less likely to be completely wiped out by fire.

Two meetings have been held and the matter discussed. About $75.00 is now available being held in several "citizens' funds," which will make quite a nucleus around which to build. For a few hundred dollars, much less than the loss by this one fire, we can secure good protection.

Tonight, (January 15th) a meeting will be had for the purpose of taking preliminary steps towards forming a fire company and becoming an auxiliary to the State Fire Association.

The Sunflower, February 19, 1901

A Fire Department has been organized and about $100.00 in cash is now in sight with some prospects of a practical system of fire protection being secured. The officers are T. J. Skidmore, President; J. F. Witheral, Vice President, W. H. Bond, Secretary and E. L. Griswold, treasurer. A double action force pump has been purchased which is now on the way and will be mounted, if it proves effective, on runners for the winter and wheels during the summer. This will throw quite a stream of water on a fire with the aid of the chemicals we now have and some hooks, ladders, axes, etc., it is hoped we can secure quite an effective fire protection. Every cottage owner should make a liberal donation to aid in this effort.

The Sunflower, March 15, 1901

With the change in the weather and prospects of the snow going off soon people are beginning to talk camp and wonder what is to be the result of the summer. There are diversities of opinions. Some think the Pan American Exposition will bring a great many visitors than on previous years while others think that it will cut down the attendance. Each side agrees from its own standpoint and makes a good case. We hope, however, that the camp of this season will equal those of recent years.

The Sunflower, May 1, 1901

A meeting of the Lily Dale Fire Company was held in connection with the Board of Directors, and Association fire apparatus was turned over to it and the tank house was given to the fire company for headquarters. It will be repaired by joint work of the Association and the fire company, the hose overhauled and everything put in order. As the water is now in the pipes and the tank kept full, we will have complete fire protection until fall when it is hoped arrangements can be made to procure apparatus which will give us protection during the winter and thus reduce our insurance rate.

The Sunflower, May 15 1901

Every spring there are dozens of letters at this office, making inquiries about the camp, and we take this method of replying to them

Cassadaga Camp is located on the Cassadaga Lakes, half way between Dunkirk and Jamestown, N. Y., on the Dunkirk, Allegheny Valley and Pittsburgh Railway. The camp season opens July 12 and closes August 25, giving 45 days of public service. People begin to arrive on the grounds May 1, and many remain through the entire season and until November. May, June and September and October are considered by the residents to be the pleasantest months of the year.

Cottages can be rented of almost any size. Prices range from $15 to $150, according to location, size and furnishings. Rooms rent at from $1.50 per week to $1.50 per day, according to location, size and furnishings. There are two hotels and several good boarding houses on the ground, the Leolyn just outside the gates, the Iroquois at the depot and Shady Side, Todd House and Fern Island House near by. Rates are from $1 to $2 per day, with reductions by the week.

We have two grocery stores, meat market and vegetable supply store on the grounds, and before and after camp, the farmers bring in fresh vegetables every day and fruits and berries in their season. During the 45 days of camp everyone who stays on the grounds is compelled to pay 10 cents daily or get a season ticket for $3.50, good for the entire camp.

The Sunflower, June 15, 1901

Cassadaga Camp Meeting
Twenty Second Annual Session
Opens July 12, and closes August 25, 1901

Cassadaga camp is one of the finest resorts to spend the summer in the United States. Nature has done great things for it, while man has changed it from the primeval forest to a city of cottages and places for both amusement and instruction.

It is located on two of the Cassadaga lakes, there being four of them, three that are navigable and connected with channels that allows the small steamers to run from one to the other.

Of course the feature of Cassadaga is its lecturers and mediums who congregate here from all parts of this and foreign countries and the investigators of all branches of psychic phenomena make it a Mecca for the purpose.

The grounds consist of fifty-two acres covered with a fine growth of shade trees consisting principally of maple, beech, birch and hemlock. The camp is divided into sections by nine streets that run east and west and three that run north and south, besides foot paths through the parks.

There are three parks, Melrose, between the auditorium and entrance; Lincoln, extending from the auditorium north past the Grand Hotel and around the shores of the lake to the bowling alley and electric light works; and Caldwell with swing, croquet grounds, etc., for the amusement of the younger generation can be found. These parks are filled with flowerbeds, nice grassy lawns, beautiful shade trees, settees and all that goes to make a delightful summer resort.

Hotels

It is said, "man esteems his stomach above all else." Whether this is strictly true or not it is certain that the cuisine has a great deal to do with the comfort at a summer resort. In this Cassadaga Camp is particularly fortunate. The Grand Hotel, South Park, Leolyn, Iroquois, Shady Side and Fern Island House as well as a number of large cottages arranged to care for guests and the restaurants supply meals and lunches at reasonable rates.

Boating, fishing, and kindred sports, as well as bathing and patronizing the toboggan slide and bowling alley, take up the time of many pleasure seekers, while those who are seeking information of Spiritualism are engaged day and night in their favorite employment, all gathering and then exchanging the result of their experience with others.

Thus the time never hangs idle on the hands of Cassadaga Camp summer visitors.

The principal place of meeting is at the auditorium near the entrance. It is built upon a side hill, with a floor 50 x 80 feet back of which are eleven rows of seats raised one above the other, making seating capacity for about 1,500 people. The rostrum is about 18 x 50, giving plenty room for speakers, chairman, band and singers and instruments.

The auditorium is not enclosed. It consists of simply a roof, supported by pillars and arranged with curtains that can be lowered to close it, when desired, and when the weather is fine they are drawn up forming an awning, making an additional space of about eight feet on each side. This can be filled with settees and additional seating capacity made.

Library Hall is used for many of the smaller meetings and classes. The Children's Lyceum meet every morning except Saturday and Sunday, the Thought Exchange nearly every evening and private classes of different kinds during the day. The Octagon is so called on account of its shape. It is used as a classroom, gatherings and for dancing school.

Lectures, Séance and Classes

It has always been the aim of the management of this Camp to present the very best thought from its platform. Its name is the Cassadaga Lake Free Association and its platform has been open for free discussion of all topics. For this reasons it has become a rendezvous for all classes of people who are interested in the progressive movement of the day. As is to be expected some "cranks" are attracted and in many cases make it amusing for the people. Other have their whims and idiosyncrasies which they take every opportunity of presenting to the public; but taking it as a whole, there is a very fine line of thought presented.

Bakery and Grocery Stores

To those whose means are limited, the cost of a summer trip frequently causes all ideas to be abandoned. For this will supply all that is needed in the way of eatables, as they carry a complete line of supplies for campers. Besides a complete line of freshly baked bread, cakes, pies, cookies, etc., baked beans, and roast meats are for sale, and canned goods of all kinds are sold at reasonable rates.

Buy your tickets, have your baggage checked and your mail addressed to Lily Dale, N. Y. There is a post office and village of "Cassadaga," which is NOT the Cassadaga Camp meeting. If you come from the east or west change cars at Dunkirk or at Falconer Junction, N. Y., near Jamestown. It is then but about forty minutes ride to Lily Dale.

Cost of staying on the Grounds

The expenses of the camp are met by the sale of privileges and a gate fee. An admission of 15 cents is charged for the day for visitors. If you come to remain several days, 10 cents a day is collected by collectors who call at all cottages each morning. Season tickets are sold for $3.50. No admission is charged at meetings. A conference is held each morning except Friday and Sunday, when the auditorium is occupied with Children's Lyceum and a speaker, respectively; lectures each afternoon and Thought Exchange in the evening, Forest Temple meeting in the early morning and evening. When we consider that 10 cents a day gives free admission to all these it speaks well for the liberal policy of the Association.

The phenomena presented at Cassadaga Camp are some of the best. Every line is represented and the attendants cannot help being satisfied with the manifestations of mediumship that will be presented.

Everything is in the line of phenomena is presented. Pictures of all classes, independent slate, porcelain, and paper writing, automatic writing, test mediumship, materialization, healing, trance, clairvoyance, in fact every phase that can be found either on the rostrum or in private.

The Association has nothing to do with the séances held by the mediums, who charge prices ranging from 10 cents to one dollar for circles and all prices for private sittings, although the average prices are one and two dollars.

The Children's Lyceum meets with the popular approval of all the children. It holds its session daily except Friday and Sunday in Library hall at 9 a. m., in the auditorium Friday morning, and in addition it gives a public entertainment in the auditorium twice each season.

There is growing interest in the lyceum and any Spiritualist who does not take an interest in it is certainly derelict in his duty. Therefore, bring your children and let them learn the lessons taught therein, as well as get a training in other directions coupled with an enjoyable outing.

Dances are held in the auditorium Wednesday and Saturday evenings. The special trains from Dunkirk and the steamer from Cassadaga bring many people from away. The floor will accommodate about twenty sets; the music is excellent and the dances are of a great amusement for both participants and the many spectators who fill the seats to watch the tripping of the light fantastic toe.

Library

Nowhere can a better feast be found for the lovers of books. The Marion Skidmore Library was founded in August 1886 by Mrs. T. J. Skidmore with a few select books by standard authors and Spiritual workers. Emily W. Tillinghast was appointed Librarian and accomplished very effective work in that capacity until the close of the season of 1897. From the few books that formed the nucleus, the present Library has gradually grown by the donations of friends and authors, entertainment's etc., to a valuable collection of choice works numbering about 1300 volumes. In poetical works, Homer, Shakespeare, Pope, Goethe, Shelly, Arnold are names of but a few upon the shelves. Many volumes, the inspired works of Spiritualists, are among them; Andrew Jackson Davis' complete works of 30 volumes, Emma H. Britten, Dr. J. M. Peebles' complete works. Moses Hull's works, Carlyle Petersilia, W. J. Colville, Prentice Mulford,

Marie Corelli, Thomas Paine, Marion Crawford, Elizabeth Stuart Phelps, Channing, Carlyle, Cooper, Joseph R. Richmond, Victor Hugo, Elliot, Bulwer, Thackery, Swedenberg, Scott and the best works of many other authors are upon the shelves.

Bath House

At the bathhouse hot and cold tub and shower baths may be taken at any hour of the day or evening. It is under the management of Mrs. A. Winchester, is kept clean and is in good order and repair.

Hotel accommodations are one of the first questions concerning any resort.

In this respect, the Cassadaga Camp grounds are especially fortunate. There are two hotels upon the grounds and five in the immediate vicinity.

The Grand Hotel is within two minutes walk of the Auditorium, Library Hall, and Octagon, where principal meetings are held.

The bandstand is but a short distance from the Grand where open-air concerts are given twice a day. Many pleasant receptions and other popular gatherings are held in the parlor, which is neatly furnished, and pleasantly situated looking out on to the lake.

The people employed for the rostrum are entertained at the Grand and the people congregate on the veranda and in the parlor and office to visit with them and discuss the doings of the camp.

It faces the Upper Lake, has about eighty rooms, wide veranda around two sides of it, and a beautiful park between the hotel and lake. It will be in charge of L. M. Worden and a corps of able assistants. Open June 7 for the season, and special low rates will go into effect. The Leolyn House is directly in front of you. It is surrounded by a beautiful grove of twenty-three acres and has the Middle Lake directly to the west and south of it. Balconies and wide verandas combine to make it a very pleasant spot to enjoy the warm summer weather, while the park just south of the hotel is always cool and inviting.

The interior has been gone over during the spring, and new paper, furniture, dinning room enlarged, decorations, etc., combine to make it one of the very pleasantest hotels that can be found.

Among the attractive pieces of decorative work is a pair of portieres, made by that marvelous worker, Mollie Fancher, who though blind and crippled is able to produce the finest kind of needle work and select colors by the aid of her psychic powers.

The Leolyn has over sixty guest rooms besides ample accommodations for the guest in other ways. It is less than three minutes walk from the Auditorium, the grounds being across the street from the Camp entrance.

A fine Aeolian Orchestrelle has been added to the attraction of the Leolyn this spring. It is a beautiful instrument and is well supplied with all classes of music, from such selections as Tannhauser to the ragtime Negro melodies.

The South Park House is also within a minute's walk of the places of meeting. It has twenty-five rooms and in on another of the little parks that combine to make the grounds beautiful. The veranda on two sides also gives this hotel a pleasant place for guests to sit during the summer evenings. The building is about to change hands but it will probably continue under the management of Mrs. N. A. Dedrick.

Shady House Summer Home is beautifully situated on the west bank of the Middle Lake, opposite the Leolyn. It is built on the plan of the Old Southern Homes, has massive pillars and wide verandas, facing the lake. It is presided over by Mrs. Densmore, who does all that is possible to make guests feel that they have reached a home and not a hotel. The wide lawn and bountiful shade make a combination that is ideal and many guests make it their summer home.

The Iroquois Hotel is located directly across the street from the R. R. station. It has twenty rooms, a fine banquet hall and will make a specialty of serving meals and short orders.

While everything will be of the best, prices have been made very low, good meals served for twenty-five cents. J. C. Scheu, Proprietor.

The Fern Island House is located about three blocks from the entrance. It is especially desirable for those who want a place away from the activity of the Camp and where nature in its more primitive state can be found. D. T. Harris is the proprietor and takes great pleasure in giv-

Iroquois Hotel.

ing his guests all the comforts of a country home life.

The Todd house is well known to all visitors to Lily Dale as "The Lily Dale Sanitarium." It has not been used as a Sanitarium recently, but its proprietor, Caleb Todd, has a number of visitors each summer who enjoy a country home with all its attendant comforts.

Restaurants

Several restaurants and boarding houses where a few guests are accommodated are quite numerous and visitors to Camp will have no difficulty in securing accommodations in accordance with their desire and pocketbooks.

The fact that we are in the midst of a prosperous farming community where fresh fruit, berries and vegetables can be had direct from the gardens each morning and the well known desires of the managers of the hotels to give the best service they can to their patrons, is alone sufficient attraction. Carriages meet all trains from the Grand and Leolyn; all are within walking distance of the station.

The Sunflower, July 1, 1901

Among the decided improvements that visitors to camp will find this season is the new telephone system inaugurated by the Cassadaga and Lily Dale Telephone Co. It embodies connection with Cassadaga village; the R. R. Station, Burnhams and then the connection with the long distance telephone will make it very convenient.

The Sunflower, August 1, 1901

The Hull-Jamieson debate was continued eight nights and attracted considerable attention. Forest Temple is the scene of a great deal of interesting phenomena, and many consider it one of the greatest attractions on the grounds. The greatest point in its favor is that it is free and open. No mater what your idiosyncrasy, you are at liberty to air it, and no matter how crude or underdeveloped, there is an opportunity to exercise whatever faculty is possessed by the individual. This gives an experience that in many cases is necessary for the complete unfoldment of the latent powers.

Todd House.

The Sunflower, August 15, 1901

The Bangs Sisters are kept busy with their painting and writing mediumship. P.L.O.A. Keeler has his hands full to attend to his slate writing and has a couple of light séances each week. The Pettibones are kept as busy as P's health will permit; W. E. Hart, Florence Hart, F. Corden White, Mrs. Bliss, Mrs. Moss, in fact all of the mediums are doing a fair business.

Dr. L. H. Freedman, "The Australian Healer" arrived and looks none for the worse for his bout with the medics during the last year. Of course, he suffered in pocket and several of the mediums have united and will give him a benefit séance in Library Hall this evening, the intention being to reimburse him for some of the inconvenience and financial loss he sustained in his fight with the medical associations last year and being imprisoned in Erie, Pa. He had no charge against him excepting that he was a spiritual healer and practiced the art of curing disease without asking permission of the medical board.

Banner of Light, August 24, 1901

The Chautauqua County Veteran Union and G. A. R. of western New York and northwestern Pennsylvania, held their annual reunion and campfire at Lily Dale, Thursday, Aug 15, at which a large number of old soldiers and their families participated. In spite of stormy weather, the auditorium was well filled in the morning, when a general conference was held, with speeches by veterans and their friends. The session was an enjoyable one, and at 2 p. m. the exercises were continued, J. Clegg Wright and Hon. A. B. Richmond occupying the platform. A touching feature of the day's program was the marching of the veterans through the grounds to the cottage of Van Duzee, a suffering comrade, who was able to give greeting from his veranda. The Meadville band headed the procession.

The Sunflower, February 1, 1902

The icemen are pleased with the cold weather. There is a good field of ice, eleven inches thick and a good demand. Wages are better this season and the men in the vicinity are correspondingly elated, while Markham who runs the icehouse here says there is a good demand for shipping. We therefore expect to see busy times out on the lake while the cold weather lasts.

The ice season is at its height at present. Almost eighteen horses are now at work filling the icehouse on the upper lake and loading cars. Sixteen cars are the most that has been shipped any day so far but it is expected that several hundred will be shipped before the season closes.

Last week we had the heaviest snowstorm of the season, eighteen inches of snow on a level, having fallen in twenty-four hours. It has been necessary to shovel off roofs and verandas, and if the thaw or rain should come on, many who have made no arrangements to have their cottages cared for, will have broken and damaged roofs and verandas. The snow was shoveled off from the roof of the Auditorium where it lay thirty-seven inches on the level.

The Sunflower, February 15, 1902

The old saying "water, water, everywhere but not a drop to drink," could with a little modification be applied to this section of the country. It would be "snow, snow everywhere and a little left to eat and burn." For the past two weeks we have been experiencing the worst storm known in this section of the county for years. Trains have blockaded, no freight trains at all until within a couple of days, coal stocks are low and with many it has been a question of keeping the fires going. Potatoes, kerosene, butter and a number of articles are strangers to our stores. The prospects are the worst of it is over, but two hours of wind would blockade this road again. It took an entire afternoon for three engines and a crew of fifty men to get a train from the north end of the depot to the south end of the icehouse, a distance of about three blocks.

The Cassadaga and Lily Dale Telephone Company has arranged to have a steady ring mean a fire alarm. This is quite an item if a fire should occur at either place as alarms could be given quickly and much more time and loss might be saved thereby.

Banner of Light, May 2, 1902

The annual March meeting of the C.L.F.A. trustees was held on the Association grounds March 27th, for the transaction of important business matters relative to the mid summer session of 1902, it having been decreed that the said session shall open July 11th, closing August 24th. The inaugural week will present as afternoon attractions, Mrs. Carrie E.S. Twing, Rev. Moses Hull and Miss Lizzie Harlow. During the closing week, Rev. B.F. Austin, Thomas Grimshaw and W.J. Colville will be the speakers. Other talent engaged for the intermediate period is Mrs. Cora L.V. Richmond, F.A. Wiggin, Lyman C. Howe, H.D. Barrett, Hon. John J. Lentz, Rev. Anna H. Shaw and probably a few more which whom negotiations are now pending.

It will be gratifying to the lover of music possessing an artistic ear to know that the celebrated North Western Band and Orchestra, whose daily open air concerts are the soul of the camp, have been engaged for the season.

Miss Margaret Gaule the popular test medium will occupy with a party of friends a cottage on Melrose Avenue, coming early and remaining until the first of September, thus assuring her frequent appearance, throughout the entire season, in public test séances.

Parker and his sister Mrs. Bowen whose inspiring and beautiful singing won such universal applause will return to Lily Dale during the month of August. Another vocal attraction will be Mrs. Ralph Ely, a soloist whose renditions met with manifest appreciation a year ago. Mrs. Ely has been secured for a portion of the coming season. The Children's Lyceum will as formally be presided over by Mrs. Peterson of Grand Rapids Michigan.

Mrs. Mary Webb Baker, well known to every reading Spiritualist, has been appointed librarian and mistress of the public reading room. Authority has been given to the president A. Gaston to have the Association Hotel, The Grand, thoroughly renovated and put in first class condition for the summer guests. From the fabled land of flowers and springs of perpetual youth, comes a gentleman of long and practical experience in business, who will have charge as manager of the Association hostelry. Prospects of a successful season were never more flattering than at present. Many cottages have already been leased for the season, some have been purchased and there is quite a stir and talk about building in the air, while inquires for accommodations are as frequent as the mail.

Our June picnic will be held on the Association grounds June 13th, 14th and 15th. Mrs. Carrie E.S. Twing, Rev. Moses Hull and Lyman C. Howe being the talent engaged for this three-day session. Recent exercises in commemoration of the advent of Modern Spiritualism were held at the Dale. Mrs. Clara Watson of Jamestown, N.Y. delivered an unusually fine address.

The sixth annual session for the Spiritualists Training School, Rev. Moses Hull President, will open the grounds, May the 13th continuing until July 10th. During July and August Prof. Lockwood and J. Clegg Wright will conduct their schools the same as last season. J.W. Colville will during his engagement here conduct classes in Psyco-Therapeutics. (sic) Numerous other attractions will be announced later.—Kate O. Peate, Asst. Sect. C.L.F.A.

The Sunflower, July 1, 1902

The prospects are that there will be several gasoline boats on the lake this summer. Leo Scheu has purchased a Truscott Launch and Wm. Steck of Buffalo, Mrs. Waldow's grandson, is expected at anytime with another; it will be placed on the lake for use of the family. The row boats which have been owned for many years by the Todd boys have been bought by S.J. Richardson and have been repaired and painted and will be rented at reasonable prices as has been the cause in the past. The Richardson boys are also considering getting tools and arranging a bicycle repair shop in the boathouse at the landing.

The young people of Lily Dale have organized a society known as the Jolly Club. They gave a dance May 15, at Library Hall, which was largely attended, many coming from away. The prospects are that the young people will take an active part in the social affairs here in the future. The boys are enjoying themselves with baseball. They have organized a team and with the newcomers have quite a good one. In fact, they win the majority of the games they play. An effort is being made to purchase uniforms and equip a team with supplies which can be kept here and thus have the necessary equipment as a feature of the grounds each season. To do this a subscription paper is being circulated and a dance was given last Friday evening at which fifty tickets were sold and quite a little sum left clear of expenses.

Bicycling is a great feature this season. Heretofore there was little riding done and many have not brought their wheels on that account. If the rain would just stop long enough for the roads to get into thoroughly good condition, it would be one of the foremost entertainments of the place. As it is the roadway between here and Cassadaga Village is usually good within an hour or two after the rain and scarcely a day passes that a party does not take the trip.

The Centennial of Chautauqua County took place at Westfield June 24 and 25. Mrs. Carrie E.S. Twing gave a very interesting address on the history of Cassadaga Camp, which we reproduce in part in this issue and will complete in the next. Those present listened it to with respectful attention and we consider it quite an item that Spiritualism was accorded as respectful a hearing as was the report of Chautauqua.

The depot has been moved and will present quite a changed appearance to the summer visitors. It has been placed about twelve feet east of the train shed which has also been moved back about four feet, the platform torn out and filled with two walks and cinders between them. This arrangement will save all travel through the mud to and from the depot, which has been so unpleasant in the past.

Moses Hull took a trip to Whitewater, Wis. On business connected with the Morris Pratt Institute. He reports the prospects for the school exceedingly bright and an assured success.

The Sunflower, July 15, 1902

The Cassadaga Camp meeting opened July 11 for its twenty-third session. The camp meeting was held Friday morning, and consisted of Pioneer Day exercises. Short Speeches were the order and the opening meeting passed pleasantly. The afternoon was devoted to a continuation of the Pioneer Day exercises with Carrie E.S. Twing as speaker. The evening reception held at the Grand Hotel provided interesting and all agreed that the camp had an auspicious opening.

Monday is always "wash day" on the grounds and the program is light. But no one must be carried away with the

Railroad depot.

idea that the program is all that is carried out on Mondays or any other day. Mediums for all phases are on the grounds and any lull in the Association program is rapidly filled by some of them. . Up to the present time there has not been a popcorn stand opened on the grounds but G.L. Bellows has built a neat little building just outside the gate where the aroma of "fresh buttered popcorn" spreads out and even makes The Sunflower force hungry.

The last session of the Spiritualists Training School was held last week. We regret to say that it is possibly the last season that will ever be held anywhere. The Training School has now ceased to exist; and its place, on Sept. 30, 1902 at the Morris Pratt Institute will be opened a grander and a larger school, to take its place. Most of the students of the Training School, and all the teachers except Hull have gone from Lily Dale. Weaver has gone to his home, in Old Orchard, Maine to prepare to move to his new home in the Morris Pratt Institute building. Mrs. Hull and Mrs. Jahnke have gone to Wenewoc, Wis. Camp Meeting.

Banner of Light, July 26, 1902

Passengers over the Lake Shore and Michigan Southern Railway, Nickel Plate Railway, Western New York and Philadelphia Railway, and western division of the New York, Lake Erie and Western Railway, change cars at Dunkirk, N.Y., and take the Dunkirk, Allegheny Valley and Pittsburgh Railroad to the Lily Dale station. Passengers over the Erie system change cars at Falconer Crossing, three miles east of Jamestown, N.Y., and take the Dunkirk Allegheny Valley and Pittsburgh Railway for Lily Dale Station.

All were captivated with enthusiasm of Miss Lizzie Harlow. Rounded out by her years of experience on the platform, she is and is not the same Lizzie she was when we knew her seven years ago. Her enthusiastic manner of working has given her a place that makes her desirable on many platforms. Mrs. Cora L.V. Richmond came as usual with her improvisations and inspiration. Filed with the fire of her experience, she always has an attentive audience of many who have followed her from child in short dresses on the platform, to maturity and are always pleased to see her.

Mrs. Clara Watson is always a favorite. She has a pleasing manner and is an especial favorite at funeral services, while Lyman C. Howe seems a part of Cassadaga Camp.

Among the prominent people who are present are: Judge A.H. Daily and wife, of Brooklyn, N.Y. The Judge has been president of Lake Pleasant Camp Meeting for a number of years and is quite prominent in his home circles. His investigation of Molly Fancher, which he has presented to the world in book form made very interesting reading and are also prominent from the fact that they are strictly true.

The philosophers' corner can be found on the southwest corner of the Grand Hotel. There, A.B. Richmond, "The Sage of Cassadaga can be found," He has delivered one address on the platform and will probably deliver another during the season, but his castle is at the "philosophers' corner." There the questions of the day, physical and metaphysical are discussed and are settled to the satisfaction of everyone. That is, everyone has the same opinion he had when he started and everyone is satisfied.

Among the well-known workers who have attended, outside of those on the regular program are Mrs. Tillie U. Reynolds, who spent several days here and charmed all who met her with her pleasing manner, and Mrs. M.E. Cadwallader who has taken such an interest in the children. She spoke several times on the Lyceum question and also addressed the children at the Lyceum.

The Sunflower, August 15, 1902

Sunday at the Auditorium, Rev. Anna Shaw gave one of her most eloquent discourses. There was hardly seating capacity and many were obliged to sit up on the rostrum.

The Sunflower, September 1, 1902

Cassadaga Camp for 1902 is a thing of the past. Not withstanding the adverse weather conditions, it was a success in most ways, and with the exception of the lack of familiar faces and the great number of new ones, it was not unlike the past seasons.

The special days were better attended this season than in former years, and Canadian Day was made especially marked by the large number of Canadians on the grounds. It ended with a banquet in the evening, at which many toasts were given and responded to by those in attendance.

As the hour grew late, and the people have so much to attend to while at camp, it was necessary to adjourn before the entire program was carried out. But it was a pleasure spot in the history of the camp, especially to our Canadian friends who were the hosts of the day.

The Willing Workers have done a good work this season and have agreed to furnish a new canvas for the Auditorium, to repair the cushions and make things more presentable around the Auditorium, provided the Association will repair and paint it. There is no question but that this will be done. They bought two pianos, one for the Auditorium and one for the Grand Hotel, and paid for them, the last being an important item.

We have just been favored with a series of clippings from the Erie Dispatch, which for downright misrepresentation (not to use the harsher but true term of falsehood) are the worst it has ever been our lot to come in contact with in a newspaper. From beginning to end there is not one word of fact, while most of the statements are too absurd to be worthy of consideration. The writer claims that a dog was sold on the grounds and was repeatedly dematerialized and the purchaser could not keep him. A mythical expose was trumped up, while there has not been a season for many years when the mediums gave as general satisfaction as they did this year. Certainly no trap door exposure took place except in the imagination of the writer of those articles. He said one of the mediums was "a lineal descendant of the Dodo." He ought to explain. Little is known of the habits of that bird, but it is supposed to have been very stupid. From the description he gave of the medium, he was far from stupid. This much is certain: The writer of those articles must have investigated "spirits out of a bottle," "hit the pipe," or else he is a lineal descendant of Annanias (sic), and he could give his ancestor cards and spades and then beat him at his own game.

Right here it will be well to add that Spiritualists should be exceedingly careful how they accept articles they find in the secular press. They are gotten up for sensation because a reporter cannot find anything sensational to write about. As an example, a story has been going the rounds of the papers regarding an individual whom it was claimed was "controlled by the devil." It told of the marvelous things

Inspiration Stump—Liberty and Truth.

he was doing. This article was started by a reporter of Dunkirk, and it referred to a gentleman of high reputation, who never has any kind of control, but the whole story was deliberately made up out of a chance remark. He was asked who his control was and jokingly replied, "I think it must be the devil." That remark has been published in many of the leading papers of the country and has been enlarged on until his satanic majesty has been represented as practically ruling over the destinies of the camp when the gentleman is present. He has been sent on mythical journeys to Europe and other foreign countries exhibiting this demonical control. The difficulty in handling such a report is that the papers, which report it, will not publish the facts later, and the only thing for Spiritualists to do when they read these phenomenal matters is to investigate them and see if they are true.

An Interesting Letter

I thought some of your many readers might want to hear from this pleasant camp, so I will endeavor to write a few lines about what I have seen and heard since I came to these grounds. Last Sunday I had the pleasure of listening to an address delivered by the Rev. Anna Shaw. The subject was, "Be True To Your own Truth." She spoke for nearly two hours to a large audience who gave her the closest attention.

Wednesday was Woman's Day, and the seating capacity of the auditorium was taxed to the utmost. Among the principal speakers were Miss Anna B. Shaw and Susan B. Anthony. The principal subject was "Woman's Equal Rights." As heretofore, I must say they are powerful and magnetic speakers. Susan B. Anthony in her old age seems to still hold her magnetic influence in pleading the cause she has advocated for fifty years, and I hope she may live till she sees her fondest hopes realized.

At the close of her address she made a request to the audience to take a vote on the right for women to vote, first from the men to show their willingness by standing up. Every man in the building stood up. After the men sat down the same request was made to the women and every one of them stood up. Susan B. Anthony said the first lecture she gave on this subject was to a large an audience as this, and she made the same request. The result was three men and five women stood up.

The attendance at Lily Dale at this present time, I find up to the usual number or larger. The weather is fine but quite cool. In the evenings an overcoat is needed. I have not given much time to the testing of spirit return, as they call it, but I did go to a trumpet séance with a friend I was well acquainted with, and I must say we got a wonderful phenomena in the way of singing. His son and wife came and sang several songs through the trumpet, and my friend being a baritone singer, the son a tenor and his wife a soprano, I must say I was highly entertained. As my friend sang his part with them the voice was natural and loud. My friends and relations talked to me through the trumpet told me their names, some from Meadville and some from Chester County, my old home. Some of them had passed to the other side of life for forty years, and related incidents that had happened that I am sure the medium did not know, in fact I had forgotten till they reminded me of it.

Change In Management Of Cassadaga Camp

For several years the regular attendants and a majority of the individual stockholders have thought it best that a change should be made in the management, believing that the possibilities of the camp were not realized and that a change might result in bringing in a new element into it that would more fully carry out the ideals and latent possibilities than was being done at the time. At the annual meetings efforts have been made to bring about this change but without success as the stock was centered in a few hands, and although the by-laws provide that no stockholder shall vote to exceed 50 shares of stock, the owners transferred their stock to others for voting purposes and the by-law was a complete dead letter, thus putting the control of all elections in the hands of a very few people.

At the annual meeting of 1902 an effort was made to overcome this and elect a new ticket that was placed in the field, but without success. The ticket was defeated by a small majority of the stock represented, but the vote showed that a majority of the stockowners, if not a majority of the stock voted was in favor of a change.

As this change could not be brought about at the annual meeting, a number of people discussed buying the stock and at their request Mrs. A.L. Pettengill entered into negotiations with A. Gaston and after considerable discussion satisfactory terms were agreed upon and Mrs. Pettengill purchased the stock owned by A. Gaston, A.B. Gaston, M.R. Rouse, F.G. Neelin and D.B. Merritt, they agreeing to resign their positions on the board as soon as the transfer of stock was made.

A preliminary meeting was held Monday, August 25, at which no business of interest was transacted and on Saturday, August 30, at 1 p.m., the meeting convened at which the stock was transferred to Mrs. Pettengill, the old board resigned and a new board was elected.

As the annual meeting had been held a new election could not be called, but the by-laws provide that a vacancy on the board can be filled by the remaining members. Four of the old board were present and the resignations of two of the absent members were accepted and filled after which the members present with the new members, Mrs. Pettengill and H.W. Richardson, transacted some unfinished business, when the other members of the board resigned and their places were immediately filled.

The new board is as follows: Mrs. A.L. Pettengill, Mrs. Minnie McKeever, Mrs. Carrie E.S. Twing, Mrs. Isabelle Bates, T.J. Skidmore, H.W. Richardson, and W.H. Mix.

Ever since the consummation of the deal all kinds of stories have been floating around from a denial of the sale to the statement that it had been bought by the Everett-Moore Syndicate who would immediately construct a trolley line from Dunkirk to Jamestown and turn it into a summer resort. It is useless to say that these stories are all dreams. The purchase was made by Mrs. Pettengill who is the owner of the Leolyn Hotel and an ardent Spiritualist, and she assures us that it is intended to retain all of the Spiritualistic features and improve upon them in every way possible. No changes will be made that will in any way detract from the place as a spiritual center, but the grounds will be improved and made more inviting. The citizens will be requested to unite with the management in beautifying the place and much in the way of grading the streets, making flower beds and in other ways beautifying the grounds will probably be done, although as no meeting has been held except a short session to make a temporary organization, no particular plans have been formulated.

The question of changing the name of the organization was brought up and discussed at some length, and it was decided to postpone the question for further consideration, when there were more stockholders present. "The City of Light" was proposed for the new name, and met with considerable favor. This would be a good name, as light is constantly spread from here. The sunflower, as the emblem of Spiritualism, is always turned towards the light, as are souls in search of light turned toward Lily Dale. "Cassadaga Camp" is now the name, and it causes much confusion and annoyance on account of the town, only a mile away, by the name of Cassadaga, and the Cassadaga Lakes, and the Burnham Station, which is the station for Cassadaga.

The board considered it best to abandon the June Picnic, it is always a big expense, and very few people consider it worthwhile to come here to attend so short a session. The regular season will be held two weeks longer than it has before, and next year will open Wednesday, July 8th and close Wednesday, September 2nd, eight weeks and one day.

The Sunflower, October 1, 1902

The work of improving the grounds and buildings goes steadily on. Many trees have been taken out and now that the ground is made smooth where they were taken away you can scarcely see that they are gone. Many more could be removed in the same locality, that is, in Melrose Park and between the Auditorium and Grand Hotel, and up to the Library Hall, and still leave all that were necessary for shade. We have so much cloudy weather that we need to let the sun shine in when it will, and dry the houses and grounds out. This is very important to health and the preserving of buildings.

The Sunflower, October 15, 1902

Improvements are the order of the day at Lily Dale, and those who come here next summer will find quite a decided difference. The grading of streets will be continued and the

Grand Hotel is receiving a new roof, (the dormers were also removed) new paint and paper and a general overhauling that will make a decided improvement in the accommodations at the hostelry the coming season.

The Sunflower, November 1, 1902

W. H. Bach has been to New York City and is now in Philadelphia. He is purchasing machinery to increase the facilities of turning work out of the office. Making the Sunflower a weekly and the increased patronage in book and magazine work necessitates the facilities to turn out two or three times as rapidly.

Albert S. Cooper has purchased the place known as the Fern Island House, on the road to Cassadaga, formerly owned by D.T. Harris. It comprises about 10 acres, all the land on the south side of the road after you turn the corner past the Leolyn until you come to the lake that Cassadaga Village is on, except the lot occupied by Carver's residence. Cooper is well known in business circles in Philadelphia being the Jr. member of the firm of Cooper Bros., wholesale Jewelers of that city. They have re-christened the place, "Edelwald on the Lake," Edelwald being a German name meaning "noble woods."

The great cry here at the present time is coal at any price which cannot be had at $17 a ton, or wood at $4 a cord the last that was sold.

The Sunflower, December 1, 1902

At last we have hard coal, it arrived about a week ago, and everyone is happy to have coal to burn. Our depot agent, Julius Paine, has bloomed out in a blue uniform, which are used by railroad agents, and we feel quite citified at the result. Acetylene gas has been placed in the Leolyn Hotel recently; every room is lighted by it. This is a great improvement and will be appreciated by the guests next summer.

The Sunflower, December 15, 1902

It may not be generally known that we have an excellent photographer located permanently here. Clarence D. Griswold is as good a photographer as you will find in the cities. He built a gallery in connection with his home, and is prepared to take all styles of pictures and finish them up in the latest and best style. Bear this in mind and when you want some pictures wait until you get here and patronize him.

Horse and Buggy circa 1890

DVAP Train on Trestle

The City of Light.

City of Light, 1903-1906

The Sunflower, January 3, 1903

Like the majority of places we have no coal and as a result all of the old wood stoves in the vicinity have been pressed into service and are doing proper duty. A few of our citizens clubbed together and were fortunate enough to secure a car of hard coal. As The Sunflower was in the deal, we were fortunate enough to secure a supply of coal sufficient to satisfy our requirements for nearly two months. This is fortunate as it would have been entirely impossible to heat the office with wood.

M.E. Carrie, a machinist from the Monotype Machine Company, of Philadelphia, has been working on the Monotype in The Sunflower office for the past three weeks. Carrie is a Spiritualist and a student in the kindred subjects, and expects to spend the summer at Lily Dale.

The Sunflower, January 17, 1903

Permit me in behalf of Mrs. Barrett and myself to extend our sincere thanks to the many friends who so kindly remembered us in our great sorrow with letters and telegrams of love and sympathy. We are unequal to the task now of responding to them in pen, but hope someday to be able to express to each thoughtful friend our appreciation of his kindness. (child killed in a carriage accident)

Gratefully Yours,
Harrison D. Barrett

Boston, Mass., Jan. 1, 1903

Announcement

The precarious condition of my health forces me to abandon work of all kinds to devote all of my energies to the task of getting well. My N.S.A. work will be preformed by our able president Thomas M. Locke. Editorial work and correspondence in connection with the Banner of Light will be attended to by competent assistants in my Boston office.

I shall seek a more equable climate at the earliest moment, and set myself to the work of regaining my health. It will be a struggle of three m0onths at least, and may consume a full year; but the object to be gained is one that inspires determination to win the fight on my part, hence I shall make the effort.

Wishing you, Editor, and all of your readers "A Happy New Year, "I am yours for the cause, Harrison D. Barrett.

Boston, Mass., Jan. 1st, 1903

We know we voice the sentiment of every reader of *The Sunflower* when we express our sincere sympathy with Brother Barrett and his terrible affliction. Loss of his dear one, sickness of Mrs. Barrett, and now his own physical condition is such that he must leave all work and devote all his energies to regaining his own health.

Yet in this, he is as ever, thoughtful of the people and in a personal letter he requests us to refrain from any specific mention of his sickness. He says: "I want healing thoughts, not thoughts of sickness thrown at me."

It is thought by many that thoughts of health sent out to an ailing person will aid their recovery. It certainly can do no harm and we can throw out our kindest thoughts for his recovery to perfect health. We know that all wish it.

The Spiritualistic world cannot spare H. D. Barrett. He is needed in its work and the world cannot fail to be benefited by the labor he has performed. His physicians say he must even refrain from letter writing and so none must feel aggrieved if a letter remains unanswered.

Let us send out our best thoughts to H.D. and M.C. Barrett for their complete recovery to health and a hope for less sorrow and pain in the future than has been their lot in the past.—Editor

The Sunflower, January 31, 1903

Many people have severe colds and are making quite a success of having the Grippe. Dr. Hyde is not home which makes it somewhat inconvenient as many of our residents feel that there is no better doctor. The Dr. and Mrs. Hyde expect to return in March or April and it would be wise to postpone any further sickness until his arrival if we must be sick.

The Sunflower, February 7, 1903

The center of all thought at Lily Dale at present is ice and fishing. The law passed last winter permits fishing through the ice two days a week during the month of February and is now in its glory. As the method is slightly strange to many, it will bear description. The method of spearing fish thro the ice was learned from the Indians so far as we are able to learn. The Indian method was to take a sack of dried or something to keep them off from the ice, cover their heads up with a fur or something that would exclude the light and then watch thru a hole in the ice until a fish, attracted by a decoy fish sunk in the water under the opening in the ice came in range, then to spear them.

The modern method looks a little more to the comfort of the fisherman, but the method is practically the same. Selecting a place where the water is supposed to be six to twelve feet deep, the fisherman cuts a hole in the ice about two feet in diameter. He has brought with him a "fish coop" that is large enough to sit down in on one side of this hole and he is soon prepared for fish—if an unfortunate specimen shows himself. The opening in the ice is under a hole in the floor of the coop, which is laid down on its side and drawn to the spot on a pair of runners that are a part of it, this being necessary as the law provides that they must be off the ice at 6 pm. The coop having been placed in position over the hole in the ice, snow is packed around the base that rests on the ice, to keep all light out of the coop. This also clears the snow off the ice around the coop thus giving a diffused light in the water. The fisherman then enters the coop and closes the door making it as dark as possible in there and with a wooden decoy fish hung on a line, in the water under the ice he waits the appearance of a muskellunge and as soon as one appears he spears him by throwing a weighted spear attached to a short handle and a piece of cord. If it strikes the fish, as it usually does, he immediately pulls his fish in before he is over the shock of the spear striking him. The spear used is an ordinary three or five tined spear but is weighted by having three or four pounds of lead cast around the shank.

The Sunflower, March 28, 1903

All of the telephone poles have been whitewashed and all the hydrants have been painted green, and the Livery barn has been or is being whitewashed.

The Sunflower, April 11, 1903

Frank Fuller has begun work preparatory to putting in the foundation of his new store on South Street where he is intending to build a modern store building thirty-foot front, forty foot deep and with a twelve-foot ceiling. This, with a twenty-four foot glass front and a space of three feet on each side that will be devoted to shelving for the display of vegetables and berries in season will make an attractive place and an improvement that will make South Street residents proud.

The Sunflower, April 25, 1903

One of the reforms inaugurated by the new management is to take away all of the shanties and sheds that have been used for storage purposes, on the east part of the grounds and prepare the ground for a row of nice cottages on that street. This is quite a venture and if it meets with the success that is hoped for it will make a decided improvement.

There will be a meeting of the C.L.F.A. in Library Hall, Saturday, May 2nd. The business to come before the meeting is in regard to a change in the name, some changes in other details of the Association and general matters of business. A full attendance of those interested is requested.

The Sunflower, May 9, 1903

What will appeal to the summer visitors more fully than anything else will be the level of the lakes. For years, especially last year the water has been so high that there has been no beach and it has made the parks damp and disagreeable in all but the driest seasons.

About a year and a half ago our local postmaster, E.L. Griswold, began to agitate the question of securing an appropriation from the State to dredge out the outlet to the lakes and thus establish a lower water level that would leave a lot of swamp and mosquito breeding places dry and thus improve the health of the community and make much valuable meadow land.

These efforts were immediately seconded by some of those who possessed some political influence and the result was an appropriation of $4,000 which has been used in dredging out the outlet and today there is a nice beach near the boat landing where it was all flooded last year. The level of the lake will be established between the present low level and the former high level, making it about one foot higher than it now is.

There is now some money left from the appropriation and we are trying to get it used to make an opening between the upper and lower lakes into "Mud" lake. As there is a channel that is partly filled with undergrowth, it is hoped that our efforts will be successful.

The Board Meeting

The regular spring meeting of the board was held Saturday May 2nd. Business of the regular routine was transacted. The barbershop was granted to William Wheeler who has had it for seasons. G.L. Bellows, known to the campers as "Our Old Popcorn Man" secured the privilege for popcorn. C.H. Payne of East Aurora was selected, as electrician and Edward Kent of the same place will have charge of the Bath House. Graham Turner is to be Superintendent of the Grounds. The Misses Mix of Sugar Grove, Pa., will be ticket sellers and Riley Johnson will be Gate Keeper.

The attendants, especially the dancers, will be pleased to know that the Northwestern Band will be in attendance. It will consist of nine members and will be the ones who took a prize a Jamestown a few years ago in a contest in which some forty bands from all sections of the country participated.

The resolution looking to change the name was carried, and we will hereafter be known as the "City Of Light Assembly." It was decided to have test mediums this season and it is expected that some of the best mediums in the country will be engaged for one or two weeks each.

The one regrettable incident of the meeting was the resignation of T. J. Skidmore from the board and his position as treasurer. He has been a member of the board and it's treasurer ever since the Association was organized in 1879. He has been one of the faithful few who have stayed by the Association through thick and thin, and his resignation, which was account of his age, and failing health, was deeply deplored by all. H. H. Skidmore was selected to fill the vacancy.

At the stockholders meeting it was unanimously decided to rename the Grand Hotel "The Maplewood."

Buffalo Courier Express, May 10, 1903

Many changes in management of Lily Dale
Mrs. Pettengill has absolute control and
will dictate policy—
will be known as
"City Of Light"

Many changes are taking place this spring in the management, appearance, and scope of the Spiritualist camp at Lily Dale. Mrs. A.L. Pettengill of Cleveland, who has long been one of the factors in the management of the Assembly, has now secured absolute control of it, having secured a majority of the stock of the Association. For the immediate future she will dictate its policy and control its work. Many changes are promised. The first of these is a change in the name. Instead of Lily Dale or Cassadaga, as the Assembly has always been known, it is to take on the name the City Of Light, if the petition which has already been made to the courts for a change of title is granted. For some weeks a large force of laborers have been at work grading the streets of the Assembly camp, building new walks, making repairs, and additions to the public buildings and generally improving the appearance and convenience of the place.

"There is a bright outlook for the coming season," said Mrs. Pettengill to the Courier correspondent. "We have arranged for the strongest attractions ever presented in the camp, most of the cottages which are for rent have already been rented, and few houses are for sale."

There is to be no material change in the religious policy of the Association, many rumors to the contrary notwithstanding. Mrs. Pettengill is a firm believer in Spiritualism, and has given much of her time, energy and ability and a large amount of wealth toward advancing its cause.

"The phenomena and philosophy of Spiritualism will remain as the foundation of the Assembly," said Mrs. Pettengill in discussing this question. "Certainly we desire no change in that particular, but the scope of the work will be very materially enlarged. An endeavor will be made to attract the attention of the thinking public by furnishing a program, which will include every domain of liberal thought. The time for such action has arrived, and we have prepared the program for the coming season with that in view."

Among the speakers for the season are Miss Susan B. Anthony, the Rev. Anna Shaw, Elbert Hubbard, the Rev. Morgan Wood, Prof. Lockwood, Francis Mason, W.J. Colville, J. Clegg Wright, Eleanor Kirk and Swami Abhendanda, while F.A. Wiggin will act as test medium for the season.

The Sunflower, May 23, 1903

The dry weather has made the roads good and there is quite a little bicycling. Several new wheels have arrived and Mrs. Blinney and J.D. Torrey have each received a new one from the factory of Latta Brothers, at Friendship, N.Y. As these gentlemen are Spiritualists, we would advise our Spiritualist friends to patronize them, as they make a first class wheel...

The Sunflower, June 6, 1903

Twenty-Fourth Annual Session Opens July 8, Closes September 2, 1903

When summer comes all who can do so leave the hot cities and towns and take a trip to the country. Even those who live in the country desire a change, and seek a place, where away from the cares of home and business life, they can find such recreation and interchange of thought as will bring them into harmony with the things of nature and make them better fitted to perform the duties devolving upon them during the rest of the year.

The City Of Light Assembly is the foremost of these resorts. It embodies all the desirable features conductive to a place of rest and recreation, and is the Mecca for the best class of people interested in the study of the occult and all lines of educational growth and improvement who find it a congenial and profitable place in which to spend the summer.

Across the bridge and near the railway station is an open tract of five acres belonging to the Association where there is a ball ground...

The phenomena represented at the City of Light is of the very best. Every line is represented and the attendants cannot help being satisfied with the manifestations of mediumship that will be presented. Everything in the line of phenomena is presented. Pictures of all classes, independent slate, porcelain, and paper writing, automatic writing, mediumship, materialization, healing trance, in fact every phase that can be found on the rostrum or in private.

The Association has nothing to do with the séances held by the mediums who charge prices ranging from ten cents to one dollar for circles and all prices for private sittings, although the average prices are one and two dollars...

The Sunflower Pagoda carries a complete supply of reading matter, consisting of all classes of Spiritualistic literature, the popular magazines, and will, as it has in the past, have a stock of fine candies, cigars, summer drinks, paper, ink, pens, the Spiritualistic papers. Etc. As in the past it will have ginger ale that has been so popular among those who are troubled by a change of food and water, and also the finest quality of unfermented grape juice. The pagoda will be headquarters for the Sunflower and will take subscriptions for all the Spiritualistic papers...

On the North end of the grounds is a fine Bowling Alley, Billiard and Pool tables. H.A. Everett, a son-in-law of Mrs. Pettengill, presented the Alley to the Association...

The first question a person will ask concerning a resort is what are the hotel accommodations and rates? There are seven hotels and one restaurant either on the grounds or within five minutes walk of them, and there are other places where a few people can be accommodated. Prices range from $4 to $15 per week, placing the range within reach of all visitors.

The Association owns the Maplewood, formally The Grand; it is within two minutes walk of the Auditorium. The South Park House is within a few minutes walk of the places of meetings. It has twenty rooms and the veranda on two sides makes this a pleasant place one may enjoy the warm weather. The Leolyn Hotel is surrounded by a grove of twenty-three acres and has the middle lake directly west and south of it. There is also a mineral spring whose waters are free to all, the medicinal qualities of which surpass those of Cambridge Springs.

The Iroquois is a licensed hotel located directly across the street from the railway station. It has twenty rooms, a fine banquet hall, and makes a specialty of serving meals and lunches. This season they will serve all kinds of cheese and meat sandwiches. The Moore Cottage has had quite an extensive experience in catering and George P. Moore will open his large cottage as a select boarding house. The cottage is beautifully situated facing the lake. Mrs. Dedrick, at the Sage Cottage, and Mrs. Conant-Pierce, on First Avenue are also prepared to care for a limited number of guests.

Shadyside Summer Home is located across the lake from the Leolyn; five minutes walk from the entrance. The house has been thoroughly overhauled, newly papered and painted, furniture and beds renovated, and all arrangements made to care for summer visitors. An excellent cook has been engaged and Mrs. Densmore and Madame Vignier intend to make a veritable summer home of it. In addition to the house they are now building a dancing pavilion, which will have a floor 40 x 50 feet, with a promenade 15 x 40 feet. A movable platform outside the floor will be provided for the music thus giving the entire floor for dancing purposes. Parties will be held afternoon and evenings when there are no parties on the grounds.

The White restaurant will be in charge of Mrs. Jennie Dayton. The proprietors Dayton and Hall, have overhauled it, painted and put in new supplies and will conduct it as a first class restaurant. Meals will be served regular, and short orders and lunches at all hours.. Prices will be reasonable. Richardson's Café is located near the Auditorium. It will serve lunches, ice cream and cake.

The Sunflower, June 13, 1903

The new sewer has been laid in Caldwell Park and they are now working on the extension up South Street. These are decided and have been necessary improvements for a number of years. This with the lowering of the lake level will make Caldwell Park a far pleasanter place the coming summer.

The Sunflower, June 20, 1903

Allen Campbell is spending his spring vacation on the grounds. He has been suffering from rheumatism and stopped in Buffalo on his way here to take baths from Dr. C. Hagen. He reports great benefit from them.

The Sunflower, July 4, 1903

The tubs at the bathhouse at the beach have been newly painted with enamel paint and the tank has been replaced with a new galvanized iron one, thus securing clean hot water. The electric lights will all be in place on the grounds and will be lighted the evening of the fourth. C.H. Payne is in charge of the electrical light plant.

Owing to the recent death of Caleb L. Todd, his late residence will be sold. It consists of the property known as the Todd House, or Lily Dale Sanitarium including a large brick house, frame barn, twenty three acres of land, with rose bushes and other shrubbery, apple, pear and plum trees; running spring water piped to all floors of the house; modern conveniences. He has about thirty rods of lake frontage and overlooks the Assembly grounds and three of the lakes. It is about forty rods from the Assembly entrance.

The Sunflower, August 15, 1903 (paraphrase)

The evening of the 4th of August the band went to the depot and escorted Miss Susan B. Anthony to the Leolyn Hotel where she was to be the guest of Mrs. Pettengill. The next morning the first meeting of the day was a symposium in which a number of prominent workers took part. Some of the women on the platform were: Mrs. A.L.Pettengill, President of the City Of Light Assembly, Susan B. Anthony, Rochester, N.Y., Honorary President of the National Woman's Suffrage Association; Rev. Anna H. Shaw, Philadelphia, Penna., Vice President of the National Suffrage Association; Mrs. Charlotte Perkins Gilman, New York City, Author and Lecturer.

Mrs. Gilman's work is principally with the family, mothers and children, and her lectures are principally concerning home life. Miss Anthony is pledged to universal suffrage, while Miss Shaw covers the entire field of human rights—woman in particular.

The Sunflower, August 15, 1903

One of our readers wants us to tell more about what the mediums are doing. We don't know where to begin. There are about one hundred mediums on the grounds. They are all giving sittings and treatments everyday. They are getting the same class of phenomena all the time and we do not know how to get up any new accounts of their work. It is old to report that _____ went to _____ and got a message on the slates from his mother in spirit life. The slate writers on the grounds get probably 30 or 40 such messages daily. There are five materializing mediums here and they hold séances three times each week. From ten to thirty forms appear each séance and the larger proportion of them are recognized by people in the audience as friends or relatives. So far as anything startling occurring, we have only heard of one: In this case the spirit reported to the sitter before he knew of her transition and he agreed to write the matter up for us and send it in so that we will doubtless have it before many issues. This is a very convincing thing.

Francis Edgar Mason is giving some of his radical lines of thought. He is striking in his statements and shocks some, amuses some, instructs some—so the world is made up. The conference meetings are more than usually interesting as they have subjects in a number of cases that add to the interest. People have something to think and thus to talk about. They are of the utmost interest as they are exchanges of thought of the different ones who come from widely separated parts of the country.

One of the more important days of the season will be Canal Day, the 22nd. The speaker of the day will be State Senator Henry W. Hill of Buffalo who will deliver an address in the afternoon. The morning will be devoted to a symposium. This is a matter of supreme importance to the people of the whole country. A deeper barge canal connecting the Great Lakes with the Hudson River will be of inestimable value to the people of New York State and the entire country. We hope for a large local attendance on that day.

The Sunflower, August 29, 1903

Canadian Day was celebrated on the 19th. Parties arriving on Canadian Day itself reinforced the Canadians who were on the grounds. The Auditorium was attractively decorated with bunting in red, white and blue, with flags showing the maple leaf, union jack and the different emblems suggestive of the different parts of the British Empire. The exercises in the morning consisted of a symposium in which eight speakers took part. The Canadians also had charge of the "Woods Meeting" at 6:30 p.m., on that day.

There was the element of harmony and good will as usual pervading in the camp on Canadian day, which seems to have become a fixture now on the program of the Lily Dale Assembly.

The Sunflower, September 26, 1903

About 1:30 a.m. Sunday, an alarm of fire was sounded and it was found that the large icehouse on the west shore of the upper lake was in flames. It was a large structure and made an imposing sight as the flames made their way thru the dry wood. Quite a few of the tools were saved but the building and the heavy tools and machinery was a total loss. Markham, the owner, was reached in Buffalo by telephone, but we are unable to learn the amount of the loss or the insurance. There was still a large quantity of ice in the building, some of which will be suitable for use. For a time it was feared there might be danger to the buildings on the Skidmore farm, but the wind was favorable and the icehouse alone was destroyed. Trains were not delayed. The origin of the fire is unknown. (Loss of the icehouse was $25,000—insurance was $17,000)

The Sunflower, October 3, 1903

A great deal has been said about a rival camp that is to be started at Chautauqua Lake by a combination headed by A. Gaston. So far as we are able to learn no special steps have yet been taken, and so far as the public is concerned the details are yet in embryo. It would not be strange if such a move was made, and if it is, there is room for all. Lily Dale has such a name that, while a camp started in opposition to it on Chautauqua Lake would doubtless receive a good support, locally, and from excursions, it would be some time before people would be weaned from Lily Dale and the accommodations would be arranged to make it a menace to the prosperity of this place. We do not say this with any malice. We have been asked what our opinion was on the subject and this is it. There is room for other camps in the State of New York…we should not think that it is aimed as a blow at this camp at all. [This camp was never started.]

Banner of Light, September 19, 1903

The mad craze for phenomena only is gradually abating, and in its stead is being instituted a deeper search for the self, a desire for greater individual growth and expansion. Mankind is slowly learning that only through the self can man truly know the self, and when this truth is fully realized and acted upon at large, the knowledge of immortality will become an inherent recognition in every human heart. A phenomenal psychic was heard to say that people were using more discernment this year than ever before, and were harder to please, which shows that phenomena, like everything else, must progress to higher states and conditions, or much of it will be left behind in the onward march.

The Sunflower, November 14, 1903

Everything is a usual here the people all seem happy and healthy, and contented to settle down for the winter without thought of being lonesome. Many people say they do not see how anyone can stay here in the winter. If you have a contented mind you are contented anywhere, and I guess the residents of Lily Dale have cultivated contented minds if they did not already have them.

"...Unless better rates can be made with the railroad than have been in the past the icehouse will not be rebuilt..."

Mrs. Pettengill our genial President has returned from her trip to Washington where she attended the N.S.A. Convention. Mrs. Pettengill is anxious that something should be going on in a social way among our winter residents and extends the free use of Library Hall for that purpose.

The Sunflower, December 20, 1903

Sunday evening, December 20th, the cry of fire was heard at quiet Lily Dale, which resulted in the complete destruction of the residence of S.J. Richardson, situated at the southeast corner of the Auditorium. The origin of the fire is unknown but it is supposed to have been due to a defective chimney. No one was in the house at the time the fire was discovered...everyone ran with their chemical fire extinguishers, pails, shovels and ladders, and a general fight ensued.

It was at once apparent that the Richardson house could not be saved and the all important thing was to keep the fire from spreading...the Richardson house was a twenty room house, well furnished throughout with 14 beds, 90 chairs, dishes sufficient for restaurant purposes, and everything else accordingly...the Auditorium was badly scorched, it being only about twenty feet from the Richardson cottage. (No other building was ever placed on that lot again due to the proximity of the Auditorium.)

The Sunflower, March 5, 1904

One by one the valiant pioneers of our cause are passing hence to the land of the ever living beyond the mortal. The latest to answer the call of the messenger is J. Frank Baxter, a name known wherever Spiritualists congregate, and wherever our gospel has been preached in this broad land...when he was about thirty years old he began to gain reputation as a lecturer on Spiritualistic subjects, and soon came to devote his entire time to that work. He made several tours over the United States and through Canada as a lecturer, singer and medium...the departure of our coworker will create a vacancy it will be difficult for the moment to adequately fill.

The Sunflower, June 4, 1904

It will not come as a surprise to our readers to learn that Thomas J. Skidmore, so long and so favorably known, has passed into the world of immortals. Sunday evening April 17, at about 7:30, he was smitten with paralysis, and from that time until the end, May 25th, he gradually declined. Skidmore was born at Lewisville, now Morris, N.Y. on October 6, 1826. His parents moved to Charlotte, when he was seven years of age, afterwards moving to Laona and Fredonia, all within a few miles of this place.

His early education was such as fell to the lot of the boys of that time, and he afterwards traveled over quite an area of the country in his search for profitable employment. The days of reconstruction gave him an opportunity for exercise of his business facilities and he became interested in railroad building, but finally devoted himself to one branch of bridge construction.

It was then quite a feat to build a bridge, as the builder was the designer and constructer, and the engineering problem to be solved was sometimes almost insurmountable. It was by his advice that the casings were used in

Thomas Skidmore.

building the bridge at Omaha and Council Bluffs, where it had been impossible to secure a foundation on account of the shifting sands of the Missouri River. They proved a success and have been used extensively in similar cases.

He was engaged in bridge construction for the government during the war, and built the "long bridge" across the Potomac at Washington. He was one of the incorporators of the Watson Bridge Company of Paterson, N.J., also one of the founders of the Fredonia National Bank, one of the strongest financial institutions of Western New York, and was a director up to the time of his death.

He was married to Miss Marion Johnson in 1854. During the early days of this organization, he was quite active and was its financial backer during the years of its struggle for existence and he and Mrs. Skidmore were always among the first to respond to any call in its behalf.

Mrs. Skidmore passed to spirit life from Cincinnati, Ohio, while on her way home from Lake Helen, Florida, February 3, 1895, since which time his brother Henry and sister Mrs. M.F. Tolles and for the past few years, Mrs. Sarah Skidmore, widow of his brother Oscar, have shared his home here. Mrs. Elizabeth Page, who was engaged as housekeeper by Mrs. Skidmore, several years before her transition, has remained in the same position all these years.

They left no children; those born, with the exception, a daughter who lived to the age of twenty, died in infancy… his knowledge sustained him and only a few days before the end came he said, in a delirium, "Marion, you and Kitty have been alone a long time, but I will join you soon." Was it delirium? Was it not a beautiful vision of the gates ajar? Did not the door to another world swing open that he might see the angel visitants, and catch a glimpse of his loved ones who were waiting? We choose to believe it such. Woman's Day 1904 the featured speakers were Mrs. Lillie, Mrs. Gilman and Helen Campbell.

The Sunflower, March 21, 1905

Mrs. Calphurina Straight niece and namesake of Mrs. Ramsdell at her home in Laona entered into peace on March 5th, just three weeks after the departure of her aunt. Mrs. Straight's age was 66 years and a few months. She along with her husband completed his earthly work three and a half years ago, was among the early workers at Camp Cassadaga, the Straight-Ramsdell cottage being one of the first erected on the grounds. Clara Watson officiated at the memorial services held at the home in Laona and the earthly form deposited beside that of her husband at the Laona Cemetery.

The Sunflower, May 6, 1905

The Association office housed in with the post office has been moved about thirty feet from its present location and will be improved with a veranda built around it on three sides. This will make a wider entrance and all agree is a decided improvement. There will also be two entrances from within and without the grounds.

The Sunflower, August 5, 1905

William Hammond signed in at the Leolyn Hotel, August 27th.

The Sunflower, August 26, 1905

Wednesday—Woman's Day was as usual the greatest event of the season. Mrs. Pettengill president of the Assembly entered and introduced two well-known characters the world over—Rev. Anna Shaw and Susan B. Anthony to the rostrum. They were hailed by a hearty round of applause, and the session was packed to the extreme. All available chairs and park sofas had to be brought into requisition to accommodate the eager, and several hundred had to content themselves with standing outside. It was estimated that 1500 were present.

The Sunflower, September 3, 1905

At the board meeting the following officers were elected: Abby Louise Pettengill-President, Henry Everett-Vice President, and E. Eustaphieve—Secretary, A.C. White—Treasurer, Laura G. Fixen-Auditor.

Trustees: Abby Louise Pettengill, Annette J. Pettengill, and Albert C. White, Henry A. Everett, Laura G. Fixen, Esther C. Humphrey, and Homer Todd.

(Notice 3 Pettengill family members were on the board)

A special stock holders meeting of The City Of Light Assembly will be held on the 18th day of September 1905 at ten o'clock at Library Hall for the purpose of voting upon a proposition to increase its capital stock from twenty thousand dollars consisting of 4,000 shares of the par value of $10.00 each to forty thousand to consist of 4,000 shares of the par value of $10.00 each and for the transaction of other business. (The Association is desirous of selling the bonds that come due in January—or did the Pettengill family want further controlling stock in the Association?)

San Francisco Earth Quake...April 18, 1906

The San Francisco Earth Quake devastated Abby Louise Pettengill's financial empire and her family's financial holdings. Most of Mrs. Pettengill's investments were within San Francisco even though she was from Cleveland, Ohio. In order to re-align her finances apparently she and her family sold their stock investments they had within The City Of Light Assembly. She, along with Everett, her son-in-law and daughter resigned from the board of directors. She kept her house on Melrose Park and the Leolyn Hotel until 1910—selling the Leolyn hotel and woods to the Assembly in 1910.

Mrs. Pettengill could well have abused her wealth at Lily Dale but chose to make it better…the preeminent Spiritualist camp of its day…

Esther Humphrey stepped up to become President, H.W. Richardson-Vice-President, Laura Fixen-Secretary, and Dr. George Warne-Treasurer, R.W. Savage-Trustee-, J.W. Stearns-Trustee- and Lee Morse-Trustee.

The Auditorium was again enlarged and enclosed, with canvas curtains lowered in bad weather. Susan B. Anthony made her transition on March 13, 1906.

The season of 1906 lasted from July 13-September 2nd. A season ticket was $4.00 and 15 cents for a day fee. Visitors were requested to pay 10 cents for each additional day to their hostess who in turn paid that to the grounds collectors. The Maplewood Hotel rates were room and board $1.25 a day for a single and $1.50 for double rooms and upwards.

At the annual meeting of 1906 the stockholders voted on changing the name of the association to The Lily Dale Assembly.

Excursion train and people walking to Lily Dale.

Afterword

The beginning of Lily Dale Assembly seemed a good place to stop writing this book. Another new era was beginning—quite possibly a much more interesting and controversial one. The "Hey Days" of Spiritualism began to subside, mental mediumship grew stronger, séances were monitored, and mediums began to be officially tested. In 1925 Lily Dale Assembly dissolved the stock corporation and became a membership corporation. Many well known and flamboyant mediums and speakers continued to serve the platform in the Auditorium, Inspiration Stump, and Forest Temple. There were good times and lean times. There were several exciting "Tipping Points." Today as in the beginning Lily Dale adheres to the Principles of Spiritualism—the pillar of strength it will survive with. The author intends to continue the history with a second book tentatively called *The Spirits of Lily Dale—Courage and Determination*. That book will span 1907 into the 1980s.

A short summary of today's Lily Dale: Many families reside here year round in the same houses our pioneers lived in. Fitted with modern amenities—quite comfortable. The children go to school several miles away at Cassadaga Valley Central School. The atmosphere is quiet. The pace much slower. The towering trees of the Leolyn Woods are much as they were in 1898, the second oldest natural growth forest in the state of New York.

As the pioneers pass on and the years go by other individuals have stepped in to fill the void. Summer camp now runs from the last Friday in June to the day before Labor Day. Some workshops continue into September. During Camp Season there is a gate fee for adults. Approximately forty registered mediums have signs on their houses who give private readings for a fee. Outside readings are free at 1:00 and 5:30 at the Inspiration Stump in the Leolyn Woods and 4:00 at the Forest Temple. Church Services are daily in the Auditorium at 2:30. The Museum, across from the Healing Temple, is open 11:00-4:00 daily. Healing services are held in the Healing Temple at various times daily.

Examples of some activities and workshops are: meditation, yoga, history tours, astrology, sweat lodge, drumming, healing, spirit walks, mediumship development, and Reiki. Many workshops—New Age and Old Age—something for everyone. Usually 100 workshops. The Lily Dale Assembly can be reached at 716-595-8721 or *www.lilydaleassembly.com*.

The author can be reached at *ronnagylilydale@gmail.com* or his website *www.ronnagy.net*.

Additional Photographs

Auditorium.

The original Fox cottage.

The channel.

Band on Stage

The Stage

RANDOLPH S. ROTHSCHILD COLLECTION
(OCTOBER 15, 2003)

Lot# 1056

1879 10¢. Judd 1584 (R-6). Silver, RE. 39±1 grains. The obverse is that of the famous ``Washlady'' design, so-called due to the somewhat tousled hair exhibited by Liberty. The central reverse reads *ONE DIME* inside a circle of beads. A curved emblem bearing the legend *E PLURIBUS UNUM* is at the upper reverse while a wreath of wheat, cotton leaves, and bolls dominates the remainder of the reverse periphery. **Gem Brilliant Proof.** Shades of rose-gold and lilac-blue accent the periphery on either side. The underlying fields are fully mirrored and nearly defect-free. Cameo devices complete the distinctive visual allure of this beauty! Quite **rare** and, without question, of the utmost importance to patterns collectors! *(cp8)(SEE COLOR PLATE)*

THE CASSADAGAN ADVERTISEMENTS.

Announcement

OF THE

SPIRITUALIST TRAINING SCHOOL.

Moses Hull, President, 72 York St., Buffalo, N. Y.
Mattie E. Hull, Secretary, 72 York St., Buffalo, N. Y.
A. J. Weaver, Treasurer, 44 Ontario St., Cleveland, O.

The Fifth Session will be held on

The Cassadaga Camp Grounds, at Lily Dale, New York . . .

Session Opens May 14th, and Closes July 12th, 1901.

COURSE OF INSTRUCTION.

Higher Criticism, Bible Exegesis and Parliamentary Law, - MOSES HULL.
Oratory, Voice and Physical Culture, Exercises in Expression,
                MRS. ALFARATA JAHNKE.
Philology, Rhetoric, Composition and Logic, - A. J. WEAVER.
Psychic Lessons and Class Sittings for Development, under
 Direction of Spirit Guides, - - - MATTIE E. HULL.
Juvenile Department, - - - To BE SUPPLIED.

EXPENSES.

Tuition for the term of eight weeks, - - - - - $6.50.
For any part of term, where whole term cannot be taken, per week, $1.00.
Board and Lodging on the Grounds, per week, - $3.00 to $4.00.
Cottages or Rooms for self-boarding at small expense.
Cost of Books, from $1.50 to $4.00.
Books can be had on the Grounds.

OBJECT OF THE SCHOOL.

To train its Students for Thinking, Writing, Public Speaking and Mediumship.

For further Information Address the Secretary or Treasurer.

EXTRAORDINARY OFFER!

Providence, January 1st, 1882.

By direction of Dr. York (MY SPIRIT GUIDE AND MEDICAL ADVISER,) I hereby agree to send postpaid to any address upon the receipt of

10 CENTS,

ONE BOX OF

DR. YORK'S LIVER AND KIDNEY PILLS,

Or 3 Boxes for 25 Cents.

Dr. York's Pills are a SURE CURE for all diseases of the Liver and Kidneys and are purely *Vegetable.* They do not contain Mercury, Calomel or any other poisonous substance.

This offer will hold good ONLY from January 1st, 1882, to April 1st, 1882, when the price will be 25 Cents, per box, or 5 boxes for $1.00.

Address JAS. A. BLISS,
17 Greenwich Street, - Providence, R. I.

FERN ISLAND HOUSE,

RATES.

Board per Week,	$7.00
Board per Day,	1.00
Breakfast,	.50
Dinner,	.50
Supper,	.40

BUSS FARE.

To Cassadaga,	$0.10
To Cassadaga Station,	.15
To Camp Ground,	.10

Dunkirk, Allegheny Valley & Pittsburg R. R.
(N. Y. C. & H. R. R. R Co., Lessee.)
Operated by The L. S. & M. S. Ry. Co. for Lessee.

LILY DALE, N. Y. to
FREDONIA, N. Y.

Returning, good only on date of sale as stamped on back.

FORM L.D.

16-8-04   2-7-06

6882

The Leolyn.

MENU.

DINNER.

Chicken Soup, Family Style

Ripe Olives   Celery   Mixed Pickles
Green Vegetables

Baked White Fish, with Caper Sauce

Roast Beef, au jus
Roast Veal with Raspberry Jam
Roast Lamb with Mint Sauce
Roast Chicken with Dressing

Boiled Ham   Boiled Tongue with Jelly

Plum Charlotte

Mashed Potatoes   New Potatoes Boiled
Green Corn   Mashed Turnips
String Beans

New Apple Pie   Custard Pie   Blackberry Pie

Gypsy Pudding

Strawberry Ice Cream and Cake.

Edam Cheese   Cream Cheese

Tea   Coffee   Milk   Iced Tea

Lily Dale, N. Y., August 17, 1904.

May G. Du Rand's Entertainment
"The Spinster's Club"

See Prof. Makeover with his wonderful remodelscope

CAST OF CHARACTERS

Character	Actor
Prof. Makeover	William Elliott Hammond
George Washington Jones	Homer Sibley
Josephine Jane Green	June Lovett
Priscilla Abagail Hobbs	Harriet Chase
Cynthia Priscilla Jones	Juanita Grogan
Ophelia Avillo Pitkins	Syble Purdy
Patience Desire Mann	Edith Griffith
Rachel Rebecca Short	Clara Haight
Sophia Bronson Titterington	Clara D. McKnight
Portia Olivia Bennett	Grace Taylor
Penelope Gertrude Doolittle	May G. Du Rand
Betsy Bobbitt	Alice Middlemas
Jemima Ball Bump	Carrie Bangs
Frances Lucretia Goodhope	Margaret Barkell
Jerushia Matilda Spriggins	Minnie Myler
Martha Elvira Blathers	Alice Evans
Florence Rebecca Corey	Elizabeth Kramer
Nerissa Ethel Bodkin	Soenya
Eliza Jane Beeswax	Laberta Hinsler
Anastasia Melissa Huggins	Mrs. Tennant
Sophronia Arminta Long	Aurora Kline
Jessica Juliet Smith	Grace Aiken
Widow Wise	Alvira Phelps
Violet Ann Ruggles	Eva Stetson
Mercy Desire Adams	Mrs. Nixon

SPECIALTIES BY

Jane Spates   Martha Wallace   The Twins
Georgianna McKnight   Gertrude Gard   Little Johnson Girl

Tuesday Eve., Aug. 5
LILY DALE, N. Y.
AUDITORIUM

8:15 O'clock   Admission 15c and 25c

THE
BROTHERS DAVENPORT

AND

MR. W. M. FAY,

Who have returned from Paris, where they appeared before the EMPEROR OF THE FRENCH and the Imperial Court, and whose Séances have excited the most extraordinary interest in the first Literary and Scientific Circles, will give a SERIES OF THEIR

WONDERFUL
SEANCES

FOR ONE WEEK ONLY!!

AT THE

QUEEN'S CONCERT ROOMS,

HANOVER SQUARE,

ON

MONDAY, TUESDAY, WEDNESDAY, THURSDAY, and FRIDAY, DEC. 18th, 19th, 20th, 21st, and 22nd.

The phenomena will occur under the close inspection of a Committee selected from the Audience by Ballot.

TICKETS at the Rooms, daily. Cabinet Séance—Stalls, 5s. Unreserved Seats, 3s. Dark Séance, 7s. 6d. Tickets for Both Séances, 10s. 6d.

CABINET SÉANCE to Commence at Eight o'clock, and the DARK SEANCE at half-past Nine.

APPLICATIONS FOR PRIVATE SEANCES TO BE MADE TO MR. ROBERT COOPER, 14, Newman St., Oxford St.

Pour les détails, voir les journaux et affiches.

à 8 heures   CE SOIR   à 8 heures

SÉANCE EXTRAORDINAIRE DE L'ARMOIRE.

PAR LES

FRÈRES DAVENPORT.

Cette séance complète la première partie du spectacle.
La seconde partie entièrement séparée et distincte de la première se compose d'une

Séance dans les Ténèbres
par MM. Fay et Ira Davenport

à laquelle on n'admettra qu'un nombre limité de personnes moyennant 2 francs extra.

Pour les prix voir les journaux et affiches.

Bruxelles, Imprimerie de PARYS, rue de Laeken, 44.

THÉATRE DES BOULEVARDS

Lundi 2 Juillet 1866.
ON COMMENCERA A 7 HEURES ET DEMIE.

PROGRAMME

PREMIÈRE PARTIE.

CONCERT DES XXV

sous la direction de M. STEYAERT.

1. La chanson des Alpes, arrangée par — Weber.
2. Ouverture les Trois Mousquetaires par — Halévy.
3. Arlequin, polka arrangée par — C. Bullinckx.
4. Grande fantaisie sur I Masnadieri (opéra italien) — Verdi.
5. Il Baccio, valse arrangée par — D. Paque.
6. Champagne, galop arrangé par — Van Loo.
Solo pour Carillon.

DEUXIÈME PARTIE, A 8 1|2 HEURES.

LES FRÈRES DAVENPORT

SÉANCE EXTRAORDINAIRE DE L'ARMOIRE.

TROISIÈME PARTIE A 9 HEURES.

Séance Célèbre dans les Ténèbres
PAR M. FAY ET IRA DAVENPORT.

Les personnes désirant assister à cette Séance paieront un supplément de 2 francs.

Brux. Imp. de P. A. PARYS, rue de Lacken, 44.

MAGGIE WAITE

AND

Troupe of 30 Artists

AT LILY DALE AUDITORIUM

Friday Eve., Aug. 16, '29

Largest Vaudeville Show of the Season

ROMEO & JULIET
BALCONY SCENE

John Slater and Maggie Waite
IN THE TITLE ROLE

Don't Miss this Great Shakespearian Act

8:15 SHARP

Adults 25 Cents **Children 15 Cents**

G. D. Foster Print, 16 W. Main, Fredonia

Golden Eagle Hotel,

D. E. CALLAHAN, Proprietor.

HOURS FOR MEALS:

Breakfast - - from 5½ to 10½ A. M.
Lunch - - - from 12 to 2 P. M.
Dinner - - - from 5 to 7½ P. M.

All Meals, Lunches, Dessert or Fruit sent to rooms will be charged extra.

Half Price charged for Children occupying seats at the Public Table.

Metropolitan Theater.

DAVENPORT BROTHERS,
Saturday and Sunday Nights.

Dinner Bill of Fare.

SATURDAY, FEBRUARY 19th, 1870.

SOUPS.
Ox Tail.   Mutton Broth.

FISH.
Boiled Salmon—Egg Sauce.   Baked Pike—Wine Sauce.

BOILED.
Corned Beef and Cabbage.   Leg of Mutton—Caper Sauce.
Tongue.   Corned Pork.
Bacon and Spinach.   Corned Beef.   Ham.

ROAST.
Shoulder of Lamb.   Sirloin of Beef.
Loin of Pork—Apple Sauce.   Pork.
Loin of Mutton.   Saddle of Mutton.

ENTREES.
Salmi of Duck.   Mutton Ribs with Mushrooms.
Hare Civet.   Stewed Kidney.
Oyster Fritters.   Broiled Mutton Ribs with Lyonaise Potatoes.
Baked Pork and Beans.

RELISHES.
Assorted Pickles.   Celery.   Cranberry Sauce.
Lettuce.   Worcestershire Sauce.
Currant Jelly.   Beets.

VEGETABLES.
Cabbage.   Potatoes—Boiled and Mashed.
Boiled Onions.   Turnips.
Stewed Beets.   Coarse Hominy.
Sweet Potatoes.   Summer Squash.
Fine Hominy.   Cauliflower.

PASTRY AND PUDDINGS.
Tapioca Pudding.   Peach Roll.
Pumpkin Pie.   Mince Pie.   Crackers and Cheese.
Lady Fingers.   Sugar Cake.

DESSERT.
Grapes.   Walnuts.   Raisins.
Almonds.   Pears.   Apples.

TEA AND COFFEE.

OLE BULL
AT THE CONGREGATIONAL CHURCH, TO-NIGHT.

Golden Eagle Hotel,

D. E. CALLAHAN, Proprietor.

HOURS FOR MEALS:

Breakfast - - from 5½ to 10½ A. M.
Lunch - - - from 12 to 2 P. M.
Dinner - - - from 5 to 7½ P. M.

All Meals, Lunches, Dessert or Fruit sent to rooms will be charged extra.

Full Price charged for Children occupying seats at the Public Table.

Metropolitan Theater.

DAVENPORT BROTHERS,

Saturday and Sunday Nights.

Dinner Bill of Fare.

SATURDAY, FEBRUARY 19th, 1870.

SOUPS.
Ox Tail.   Mutton Broth.

FISH.
Boiled Salmon—Egg Sauce.   Baked Pike—Wine Sauce.

BOILED.
Corned Beef and Cabbage.   Leg of Mutton—Caper Sauce.
Tongue.   Corned Pork.
Bacon and Spinach.   Corned Beef.   Ham.

ROAST.
Shoulder of Lamb.   Sirloin of Beef.
Loin of Pork—Apple Sauce.   Pork.
Loin of Mutton.   Saddle of Mutton.

ENTREES.
Salmi of Duck.   Mutton Ribs with Mushrooms.
Hare Civet.   Stewed Kidney.
Oyster Fritters.   Broiled Mutton Ribs with Lyonaise Potatoes.
Baked Pork and Beans.

RELISHES.
Assorted Pickles.   Celery.   Cranberry Sauce.
Lettuce.   Worcestershire Sauce.
Currant Jelly.   Beets.

VEGETABLES.
Cabbage.   Potatoes—Boiled and Mashed.
Boiled Onions.   Turnips.
Stewed Beets.   Coarse Hominy.
Sweet Potatoes.   Summer Squash.
Fine Hominy.   Cauliflower.

PASTRY AND PUDDINGS.
Tapioca Pudding.   Peach Roll.
Pumpkin Pie.   Mince Pie.   Crackers and Cheese.
Lady Fingers.   Sugar Cake.

DESSERT.
Grapes.   Walnuts.   Raisins.
Almonds.   Pears.   Apples.

TEA AND COFFEE.

OLE BULL
AT THE CONGREGATIONAL CHURCH, TO-NIGHT.

Anyone Will Tell You

When you reach camp you will be hungry and tired. You will find good meals and beds at the

JACKSON :-: COTTAGE

11 Third Ave., Lily Dale, N. Y.

For particulars and program, address with stamp.

A. H. JACKSON, Proprietor

JACKSON COTTAGE.

RICHARDSON COTTAGE.

S. J. Richardson,

ONE OF THE MOST

Successful Healers of the Age

Is now located at his new home, ...

10 Melrose Park,   Lily Dale, N. Y.

Magnetized Flannel Sent by Mail.

The - Fern - Island - House.

The most beautiful location on the shores of Cassadaga Lakes. Five minutes walk from the entrance to Cassadaga Camp Grounds. Free use of boats to guests. Free buss to and from depot. Boat landing at the house. Good accommodations. Rates $1.00 per day. Special rates by the week.

D. T. HARRIS, Prop.,   Lily Dale, N. Y.

THE TODD HOUSE,

A FEW MINUTES' WALK FROM

Lily Dale Station,

IN SIGHT OF

C. L. F. A. CAMP GROUNDS.

Accommodation for 50 Guests.

The Best Location on the Lakes, Elegant Table, Home Comforts, Boats to be Had at any Time, Transportation to and from Trains.

Terms, $1.00 to $1.50 per Day, According to Location of Room.

HOUSE OPEN ALL SUMMER.

People Desirous of a Pleasant Summer Home, still be in Walking Distance of the Camp, yet Free from the Excitement, Will Find this a Desirable Location.

G. TODD, LILY DALE, N. Y.

CASSADAGA HOUSE,

CASSADAGA, N. Y.

First-Class Sample Room and Billiard Parlor Attached.

Steamers Run to Camp Ground in Connection With this Hotel.

CATERING TO COMMERCIAL MEN A SPECIALTY.

'BUS TO ALL PASSENGER TRAINS.

GOOD LIVERY ATTACHED.

Ample Accommodations for Any Reasonable Number of Guests.

VAUDEVILLE!

ENTIRELY NEW--BEST YET

Original Pantomime & Farce

BEWILDERING STAGE MAGIC

TO BE GIVEN BY

PROFESSIONALS

AT

LIBRARY HALL, LILY DALE,

WEDNESDAY, SEPT. 23rd., 8 P. M.

Programme

PART I

PANTOMIME SONG and STORY under direction of Mrs. McCaslin	I Lehla Walla	McCaslin
	II Sale of the Bachelors	Selected
Stage Magic		Wm. F. Keeler
Vocal Solo		E. Merle Williams

PART II

A PLEASANT PRESCRIPTION

One Act Farce, written by - M. McCaslin.

Cast of Characters	Peter Geranium	L. Allen Darling
	Peter Garlick	C. Manykin
	Rose Greenleaf, M. D.	Ella R. Williams
	D. E. D. Greenleaf	A. N. Skelyton

ADMISSION { ADULTS - 15 Cents
CHILDREN 10 Cents

IF YOU WANT A GOOD LAUGH

— COME TO THE —

Spinster Convention

And see the Old Maids transformed into beautiful young Maidens before your own eyes at

The Auditorium

Friday Evening, Aug. 21

Under the direction of STELLA M. PEET.

CAST OF CHARACTERS

Josephine Jane Green, President of the Young Ladies' Single Blessedness Debating Society	Mrs. Harriet Duhl
Priscilla Abigail Hodge, Secretary	Mrs. Mary A. Stein
Calamity Jane Higgins, Treasurer	Ella R. _____
Rebecca Rachel Sharpe	Mrs. Mary A. Sinclair
Tiny Short	Mrs. Effie Maltby
Mary Ann Fuddler	Mrs. Hattie Haynes
Jerusha Matilda Spriggins	Mrs. Florence Green
Patience Desire Mann	Mrs. Susanna Harris
Sophia Stuckup	Mrs. Seymour
Juliet Long	Mrs. Deveral
Betsy Bobbett	Mrs. Ida King
Charity Longface	Mrs. Hattie Reimmer
Cleopatra Belle Brown	Miss Celia Carpenter
Polly Jane Pratt	Mrs. Grace Hall
Violet Ann Ruggles	Miss Laverna Maltby
Belinda Bluegrass	Mrs. Irene Bailey
Frances Beauty Spot Temptation Touchmenot	Mrs. Elizabeth Cooper
Hannah Biggerstaff	Mrs. Antoinette Muhlhauser
Professor Makeover	Mr. Allen Campbell
The Professor's Assistant	Mr. Earl Keeler

ACT I. Convention Hall.
ACT II. Professor Makeover's Study Hall.

Specialties by Miss Laverna Maltby, Little Miss Fisher, Mr. Lilly, Miss Helen Smith, Miss Stella M. Peet and other members of the cast.

ADMISSION - - 25 CENTS

May G. Du Rand's Entertainment

"The Spinster's Club"

See Prof. Makeover with his wonderful remodelscope

CAST OF CHARACTERS

Prof. Makeover	William Elliott Hammond
George Washington Jones	Homer Sibley
Josephine Jane Green	June Lovett
Priscilla Abagail Hobbs	Harriet Chase
Cynthia Priscilla Jones	Juanita Grogan
Ophelia Avillo Pitkins	Syble Purdy
Patience Desire Mann	Edith Griffith
Rachel Rebecca Short	Clara Haight
Sophia Bronson Titterington	Clara D. McKnight
Portia Olivia Bennett	Grace Taylor
Penelope Gertrude Doolittle	May G. Du Rand
Betsy Bobbitt	Alice Middlemas
Jemima Ball Bump	Carrie Banga
Frances Lucretia Goodhope	Margaret Barkell
Jerushia Matilda Spriggins	Minnie Myler
Martha Elvira Blathers	Alice Evans
Florence Rebecca Corey	Elizabeth Kramer
Nerissa Ethel Bodkin	Soenya
Eliza Jane Beeswax	Laberta Hinsler
Anastasia Melissa Huggins	Mrs. Tennant
Sophronia Arminta Long	Aurora Kline
Jessica Juliet Smith	Grace Aiken
Widow Wise	Alvira Phelps
Violet Ann Ruggles	Eva Stetson
Mercy Desire Adams	Mrs. Nixon

SPECIALTIES BY

| Jane Spates | Martha Wallace | The Twins |
| Georgianna McKnight | Gertrude Gard | Little Johnson Girl |

Tuesday Eve., Aug. 5

LILY DALE, N. Y.

AUDITORIUM

8:15 O'clock   Admission 15c and 25c

The Captain Returns
A One-Act Play
AND
The Street Singer
A Four-Act Play
By MARY RIDPATH-MANN

Lily Dale Auditorium, Thursday, Aug. 25, 32
AT EIGHT O'CLOCK

CAST
The Captain Returns

DEEMS BENTLY, University Professor of
    Psychology - - - - Justin Titus
LORD HESPELER, of the War Cabinet - Arthur Meyers
CAPT. TAYLOR HESPELER, his son - Bernard S. McMahan
BANKS, the family butler - - Frank Ceney

Time: December, 1917
Place: England
Scene: Library at Hespeler Park

CAST
The Street Singer

ROBERTA HILDRETH, an American woman
    living in Florence - - Mary Ridpath-Mann
CAREY HASTINGS, an American Attorney - Justin Titus
CARLOTTA GALLI, a young Artist - Helen Fluker
    and
BENITO ROSSI, an Italian Street Singer - Arthur Meyers

Time: Present
Place: Italy
Scene: Roberta's Studio-apartment in Florence

COME ONE   COME ALL
Tickets 25 cents   Children 15 cents

Mrs. Mann begs to acknowledge the courtesy of the management of the Capitol Theatre and of Geo. H. Graf & Co., Inc., of Dunkirk, N.Y., for the loan of the Stage Setting; of Mr. Homer W. Sibley who assumed the Stage Direction, and of the Culver and Jordan Orchestra which furnished the music.

REMEMBER THE DATE!   COME EARLY!

Have you listened to the songs the Stars sing?

BOSTON LADIES' SCHUBERT QUARTETTE
MINNIE SCOTT, - - - - First Soprano
JENNIE B. WORSTER, - - Second Soprano
IZETTA B. HOLWAY, - - - - Alto
ANNA L. WHITCOMBE, - - - Contralto

City of Light Assembly, July 29 to September 2
Every one is a Finished Artist

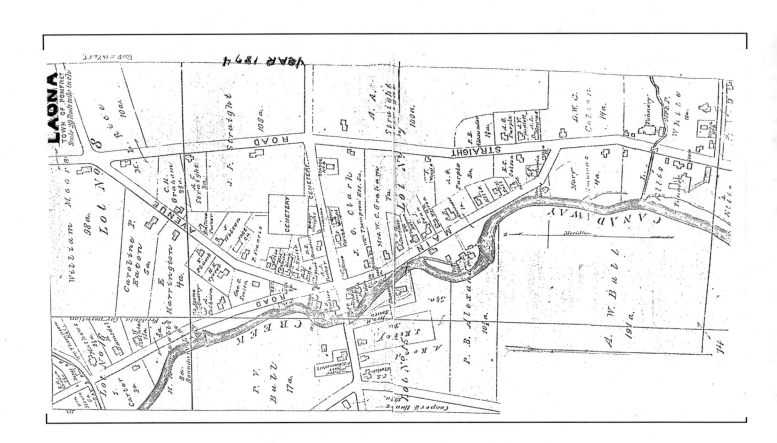

Resources

Buckland, Raymond. *The Spirit Book: The Encyclopedia of Clairvoyance, Channeling, and Spirit Communication.* Visible Ink Press, 2006.

Buckland, Raymond. *Buckland's Book of Spirit Communications.* Llewellyn Publications, 2004.

Buescher, John. *The Other Side of Salvation.* Skinner House Books, 2004.

Cross, Whitney R. *The Burned-Over District.* Cornell University Press, 1950.

LDA Chronicles. Joyce LaJudice/Ron Nagy collection.

N.S.A.C. Spiritualist Manual. National Spiritualist Association Of Churches, 1975.

To order additional copies of this book,
please send full amount plus $5.00 for
postage and handling for the first book and
$1.00 for each additional book.
Minnesota residents add 7.125 percent sales tax

Send orders to:

Galde Press, Inc.
PO Box 460
Lakeville, Minnesota 55044-0460

Credit card orders call 1–800–777–3454
Fax (952) 891–6091
Visit our website at *www.galdepress.com*
and download our free catalog,
or write for our catalog.